"WHEN IT COMES TO TEXAS FOOD, JOHN DeMERS GETS IT. HE KNOWS THAT THIS CUISINE IS NOT ONLY THE CLASSICS MADE HERE FOREVER BY NATIVES AND OUR EARLIEST SETTLERS BUT DISHES FROM ETHNIC GROUPS THAT ARRIVED THE DAY BEFORE YESTERDAY. SOMETIMES IT GETS WILD, AND SOMETIMES IT GETS MESSY, BUT THERE'S ALWAYS A BIG HEART AND A BOLD SPIRIT IN TEXAS FOOD."

– *CHEF DEAN FEARING, Fearing's at the Ritz-Carlton, Dallas*

••

"JOHN DeMERS WASN'T BORN IN TEXAS BUT HE GOT HERE AS QUICK AS HE COULD AND WE'RE HAPPY ABOUT THAT. HIS INVOLVEMENT IN THE CULINARY INDUSTRY IN TEXAS HAS BEEN A REAL ASSET."

– *TOM PERINI, Perini Ranch Steakhouse, Buffalo Gap*

••

"WITH HIS YOUTH IN LOUISIANA AND HIS MATURITY IN TEXAS, JOHN DeMERS DIDN'T STAND A CHANCE OF LIKING ANY FOOD THAT WAS BORING. AND WHEN HE VISITS ME IN CHICAGO, HE HAS A PASSION FOR MY FAMILY'S GREEK COOKING AS WELL AS FOR MY WIFE'S ITALIAN FLAVORS—A CLEAR SIGN OF ABOVE-AVERAGE INTELLIGENCE. JOHN IS A GOOD GUY WHO RELISHES GOOD FOOD, AND HE LOVES TO TELL US ALL ABOUT IT ON THE RADIO AND IN THIS BOOK."

– *CHEF JIMMY BANNOS, Heaven on Seven and The Purple Pig, Chicago*

••

"TEXAS IS A LAND OF MANY CUISINES, AS I LEARNED DURING MY OWN VENTURES AND ADVENTURES THERE—INCLUDING ITALIAN CUISINE FROM MY OWN SICILY TO THE NORTHERN EDGES, WITH A UNIQUE AND LOCAL GULF COAST HYBRID SOMEWHERE IN BETWEEN. JOHN DeMERS NEVER GETS TIRED OF TRACKING DOWN ALL THESE VARIATIONS AND ENCOURAGING THE REST OF US TO JOIN HIM FOR DINNER."

– *PIERO SELVAGGIO, Valentino, Santa Monica*

bright sky press
HOUSTON, TEXAS

2365 Rice Blvd., Suite 202
Houston, Texas 77005

ISBN: 978-1-939055-82-8

10   9   8   7   6   5   4   3   2   1

Library of Congress Cataloging-in-Publication Data on file with publisher.

Editorial Direction, Lucy Herring Chambers
Editor, Eva J. Freeburn
Design, Marla Y. Garcia

Printed in Korea through Four Colour Print Group

THE Delicious Mischief TEXAS COOKBOOK

100 Favorite Recipes from 25 Years of Eating & Drinking on the Radio

JOHN DeMERS

bright sky press
HOUSTON, TEXAS

MY WIFE LINDY AND I FIRST MET JOHN DeMERS, and first heard about his *Delicious Mischief* food and wine radio program, only a few weeks after his move to Texas in early 2001. If my memory serves, all he had to drink that day was a Coke.

We'd invited John to tour our mother ship, the original Spec's store on Smith Street in Houston, simply to make sure he knew the kinds of things we were doing. I felt sometimes back then—and I *still* feel sometimes—that journalists like John get a press release from some other food or wine retailer announcing that some new wonderful thing is finally available in the local market. And that becomes the story, even when we've been carrying the same item for months, even for years. When it comes to our competition, I've always believed that anytime anyone raises the bar of how Texans eat and drink, we at Spec's will get our share of that business. But since John was new in Houston, and indeed new to our Lone Star State, I hoped he would come to better understand our role in the process.

At his request, we plied him that day with a hot pastrami sandwich in our deli, a very popular part of our downtown store, and chatted over that Coke about everything he wanted to accomplish as the new food editor of the *Houston Chronicle*. Clearly, John was energized by the work and the opportunity that had been handed to him, especially after food editor Ann Criswell achieved such legendary status during three decades-plus holding the job. We'd known Ann, of course—nobody who loved food and wine in Houston *didn't*. Now we wanted to get to know John, recently arrived from his food-crazed hometown of New Orleans.

Lindy and I certainly enjoyed our visit over lunch, giving John the basic history of her father—Carroll B. "Spec" Jackson—starting the business as a single liquor store back in 1962. And we told him how Spec had resisted the whole "wine thing," being a dyed-in-the-wool liquor guy, until Lindy and I threw ourselves into learning about what we saw as the next big opportunity. As the years passed, not only would Spec's Liquor Store evolve into Spec's Wines, Spirits & Finer Foods, but we, our daughter Lisa and our ever-growing staff would travel to practically every country on earth meeting with winemakers and tasting their wines. In the process, we would expand to more than 200 stores, in our homebase of Houston, and in Austin, San Antonio and Dallas, as well as many smaller Texas cities and towns.

Most of that was in the future, though, as our lunch with the new *Chronicle* food editor started to wind down. Only then did John let on, almost as though it were a secret, that he still drove to New Orleans every weekend. Yes, his family was still there, waiting to make the move permanent. But also, his radio show, *Delicious Mischief,* was still there. John hosted the hour live in a studio each Sunday morning before hitting I-10 for the six hours back to Houston. One of his sponsors was the Robert Mondavi Winery, a brand we and everybody else sold a lot of, plus a popular wine retailer in New Orleans. Perhaps without thinking, I told John: "Well, you get a show like that over here and we'll sponsor it."

John did, and so we did. And John keeps on hosting the show, more than a decade after leaving the *Chronicle* to concentrate on radio and fast approaching his twenty-fifth anniversary on the air. It's been quite a ride, especially as we at Spec's expanded our reach beyond Houston in ways our founder couldn't have imagined. Indeed, with our sponsorship, John has been able to expand *Delicious Mischief* in ways he couldn't have imagined.

Along the way, we've all had to learn a lot about a lot of strange things—websites, blogging, e-blasts and 24/7 social media among them. Yet we still believe, and still devote our primary energies, to that moment a customer walks into one of our stores and asks us to help him or her find something special. John and *Delicious Mischief* help encourage folks to walk in. I feel good about the ability of our people to take it from there.

DELICIOUS
MISCHIEF & ME

"WE'LL PAY YOU."

Those words, spoken 25 years ago against the hush of the now-departed, red-velvet Sazerac Restaurant in my hometown of New Orleans, would for the first if hardly the last time change my life. I had been invited to lunch by a radio station manager, somebody I'd worked with on various events and promotions, and he had just suggested I might be good at hosting my own food and wine show on his station. Until those fateful words, however, I had a thousand reasons I couldn't do what he was proposing—I had a fulltime job, I wasn't some *disc jockey* and, most of all, I was *much too shy.* Once he mentioned there was money involved, I, with some vision of my four children in mind, was putty in his nefarious hands.

Thanks to that guy and that day's lunch, hosting a weekly radio program about food and wine has turned out to be the single best part of my working life. That manager *saw* me on the radio, before I knew enough to see myself.

There is the little matter of my parents, which might have given a smarter person a clue. There was my father, a quiet, serious high school science teacher who, in search of a better income for his family, ended up selling vacuum cleaners door-to-door, managing an auto parts store and eventually spending more than four decades as an insurance salesman. And there was my mother, a quiet, serious high school English teacher, who loved, read and even wrote poetry, though I never got to see a word of it. Had she not passed away when I was sixteen, who knows—she might have become a standup comic or, even better, a part-time burlesque artist or itinerant circus performer. Had she done any of those things, I would have known for sure what was in my future, for doing radio combines all those skills.

Most of all, however, my parents gave me my career in the way they loved to cook, eat and drink. This was New Orleans, after all, which devotes more than a little of its life to thinking about and talking about food and beverage. That cuisine-crazed culture made it inside our door, at least as far as our kitchen. It was there, I remember, that my parents truly *lived* for me—their table piled high with weathered cookbooks, mostly about New Orleans, their conversation enlivened by swigs from cans of Dixie beer. "Can you believe how much celery this uses?" seems, to me, an entirely appropriate sound bite from their years of turning pages, part of our family's nightly chatter.

My parents cooked. Every night. In those days, if people in New Orleans went to a restaurant even once a week, it was Friday for seafood at the lakefront or Saturday for steak, and they were surely celebrating something. There were no "fast food" or "casual" places (or for that matter, no microwaveable entrées) that would later blur the lines by appearing to compete on price. So my parents cooked, from scratch, all the time. And I don't recall them ever arguing in the kitchen, even about how much celery to use.

A word about their drinking, for it does figure into my story as a radio host, cookbook author and professional "food and wine guy." Looking back through the suggestive leer of TV's *Mad Men*, I'm actually surprised how little hard liquor they consumed. I don't know if they ever made *anyone* a cocktail, unless you count the "Scotch and water" my Dad sipped occasionally, the Scotch not in the least "single-malt" and invariably the cheap store brand with the purple label from my hometown's now-departed K&B drugstore. Mostly my parents drank beer, my Dad especially, nearly always cheap local beer—and that meant Dixie as the other New Orleans breweries like Falstaff and Jax shut down one after the other. They liked to drink wine too—talk about a time capsule there. Large bottles, some might say "jugs," of only two wines took up residence on our kitchen counter: Gallo Hearty *Burgundy* and Almaden Mountain White *Chablis*. Those are two inexpensive wines from California, both named after famous wine regions of France. Ah, those were the days.

When I came home from school one afternoon to learn that my mother had died, I couldn't begin to understand how many things would change, almost immediately. For one thing, or maybe three things, cooking, eating and drinking lost all interest to my father. He didn't care if he ever did those things again, because they all were part of *her*. That meant my two siblings

On my tricycle in New Orleans; on the front stoop with my mother, father and sister.

With a basket of seafood in New Orleans; with a view on the isle of Capri.

and I had to find our own dinner, and that meant that I, as the eldest, would quickly figure out how to turn on the stove. Over time, even my father warmed to the meals I put out: fried pork chops, bright orange macaroni and cheese from that blue box, beans or corn or peas from that Green Giant. And I learned the most profound lesson I ever would or could learn about food, one that's helped me survive even friendships with famous, egomaniacal chefs: It matters less *what* you serve than *that* you serve. It's the *giving* of food and drink that creates a relationship. Anything else, as we learned to say in New Orleans, is gravy.

Even living among gumbo, étouffée and spicy boiled shrimp piled on yesterday's edition of the now-departed *States-Item*, I required one other thing to turn my practical skills into something resembling a religion. And that was discovery of a much larger world—a mission I embarked upon within about 38 seconds of picking up my college degree. New Orleans, we all understand now, was a small town. Growing up, we heard of big cities like New York, Chicago and San Francisco, but no one we knew ever actually went there. And we heard too, this being New Orleans, that so-and-so's ancestors had come over from France. Still, the nine months I spent living on almost no money in Europe in 1974 and the only slightly better bankrolled six months in 1976 changed everything I knew, thought and felt about food and wine.

For the rest of my life, anytime I hear someone boast about how much his fancy restaurant dinner costs or that he has just popped the cork on the only bottle of some $3,700, highly allocated Napa Cabernet the winemaker personally autographed, I think back to those people who loved good food and good wine before *we* even existed as a nation, and I am healed. What I saw, in big cities like Paris or Rome but even more in every village whose name I couldn't pronounce across France, Spain, Italy and Greece, was people who genuinely loved food and wine, who grew and made a lot of it themselves and who saw absolutely no justification for pretense or snobbery. Everything those villagers ate back then (though not so much anymore) came from somebody they knew personally, probably a relative. It was simply the way things worked, the way they'd always worked and the way they surely always would.

Today, when I listen to some blogger/hipster/hotshot boast how much he paid for the locally grown organic tomato from the farm just up the highway by way of the farmers market just down the street, or that it's worth every extra dollar for that single perfect egg from chickens happily ensconced around the corner, I understand sadly that this is exactly *nothing* like the real life I encountered in the Old World.

Little did I know, sipping my pre-Starbucks cappuccino at some sidewalk café, that marriage, children, fulltime employment by corporations and more than one house in the suburbs were in my future. If I'd known that, I would have been happy, for nothing ever meant as much to my personal or professional life. But I didn't know. And I also didn't know how much change would befall my chosen profession, that of a reporter and editor for daily newspapers.

Three layoffs later, I can now see what none of us then *could* see, as we imagined our America forever stepping out onto the porch with its morning coffee and searching for the ink-on-paper news that some neighborhood kid tossed from his bicycle. I loved journalism then, and I still do. I loved newspapers then, and I still do. But as we struggled each midnight to wrestle the state of the universe onto the presses, not one of us could foresee a world in which most would prefer to receive our labors without ink or paper at all. And certainly no one could foresee a nation of news consumers unwilling to contribute 25 cents, 10 cents or even 1 cent toward paying us to give them all of that.

Going for a ride near Big Bend National Park; harvesting Texas grapes for wine.

So it was, against this backdrop of journalism for newspapers, magazines, wire services and books, that I ventured onto the radio. It was—and like everything else I've mentioned so far, I really *should* have guessed—love at first talk.

Radio was, as more than one station has tried to remind us over the years, "the soundtrack of our lives." Much of what we knew about our teenage years in mid-20th century America, including what songs would define us, first came into our lives over the radio. And it didn't hurt that the New Orleans talk station I started on (WTIX) had years earlier been the music station I'd listened to for all the latest from the Beatles, the Beach Boys and the Dave Clark Five.

Turns out (I learned such things in grad school, once "journalism" had upgraded itself to "communications"), radio is the most democratic of all traditional media. It requires no literacy, you don't pay for its programming and the actual delivery system—a radio—is one of the cheapest bits of technology on the planet. In Third World countries, radio to this day is the primary news source, even as the Internet makes headway.

Those great radio comedies and dramas of the 1930s understood this power as "theater of the mind" and made tremendous use of it. Just ask the thousands who fled their homes after Orson Welles' "War of the Worlds" broadcast. Will Rogers understood it too, making him the folksy hero of the common man after the Depression turned so *many* into common men. And so did Franklin D. Roosevelt, whose reassuring "Chats" were actually less Fireside than *Radioside.* Radio played in our ears throughout the 20th century in America, even when there was no actual radio nearby.

For some reason, this same newspaper writer who feared nothing as much as an empty sheet of paper found an empty hour of radio the coolest thing ever. Radio was fun. Radio was easy. And like all true journalists (other than the favored few in New York or Washington that everybody thinks we *are*), I have always identified with all worker bees. Having worked every night, weekend and holiday at least a few times, we forever feel kinship with city cops, state troopers, sheriff's deputies, firefighters, hospital nurses—everyone sipping lousy coffee instead of champagne. And having been the "talent" of our own radio broadcasts, we also respect and admire the bleary-eyed techno-souls who keep us on the air after twelve hours running all five stations in our group. Those guys are still there, sort of, still drinking the lousy coffee possibly brewed in 1983, even as business consolidation and computers eat away at their jobs.

I might, at the start, have wished to not live long enough to see automated radio; but I have lived. And really, it hasn't taken that long. Fortunately for our country, most of those other, more essential night owls remain, along with the journalists ready to chase down the highway after them, now with their laptops and iPhones standing ready.

From the very beginnings of *Delicious Mischief* (more about the name in a bit), I sensed that I was somehow different from what people seemed to expect. Even in New Orleans, with its downhome unadulterated lust for everyday eating and drinking, people expected me to be, well, classier. *Fancier.* Perhaps more pompous? After all, eighth-grade-dropout waiters looked down on blue-blooded diners in all the fine restaurants, and you don't even want to know what those French-accented sommeliers were thinking. I knew, because I knew *them,* and part of me wanted like mad to measure up. But I also knew my life so far, with parents who laughed (and yes, drank) their way through fixing dinner and with what felt like a thousand generations of European peasantry enjoying what struck me as The Good Life. There's food and there's wine, and for a brief splash of time, there's you and me. What's the big deal, people? Somehow, this attitude I didn't even know I had

At a gala with Carolyn Farb and Damian Mandola; on the air live in Houston; at dinner with the Most Interesting Man in the World—and his wife.

Live broadcast from harvest at Messina Hof in Bryan; John with the news team with UPI in New Orleans.

became my show.

For a year or so, I sneaked out of my fulltime job at lunch Monday through Friday to race to the station, first for thirty minutes and then for a full sixty. And then, when that station changed to all-blues with no notice, I convinced some other station to pay me a few bucks for a weekly hour. After that ended, I convinced another station. Yes, you are spotting a radio theme here. And since each station put its own identity into the title, the show's name changed each time a station kicked me up the street. After a few of these traumas, I remember describing what I did to somebody who'd never listened, trying to capture the irreverence and fun. "It's kinda like 'malicious mischief,'" I heard myself pronounce, recalling a legal term from some news story I'd written. And then I stopped. "Except in my case," I couldn't help smiling, "it would have to be *Delicious* Mischief."

Naming was the first step I ever took toward owning my own radio show, toward being an entrepreneur rather than a part-time station employee. It may well have been the first step I ever took toward owning *myself*.

Even as my newspaper career carried me to the *Houston Chronicle* (one of those offers you can't refuse, updating the weekly food section after the legendary Ann Criswell's three-plus decades) and even as our three daughters and one son got bigger and better, radio never ceased to be a major part of my life. I needed it. I wanted it. I loved it. And while that manager's initial promise of "We'll pay you" had morphed into far more complicated bookkeeping, there *was* a bit of money to be made.

From Day One, I've been on the air in Texas because of John and Lindy Rydman of Spec's Wines, Spirits & Finer Foods, the now-mammoth retailer that was centered in and around its Houston home in those days. Shortly after I joined the *Chronicle*, John and Lindy invited me to lunch in the deli of their main store. And as much as I enjoyed their hot pastrami and cheese sandwich,

I enjoyed their company even more. Just to make conversation, I told them about the little radio show I had back in New Orleans that kept me "going home" every weekend. "Now," said John, "you get a show like that here and we'll sponsor it." Even more amazingly, when I pulled together the numbers to produce *Delicious Mischief* in a much larger radio market, the Rydmans did exactly that. I've been on the air in Texas ever since, growing to Austin then Dallas then San Antonio, never without Spec's. The fact that winemakers, distillers and brewers from every corner of the globe visit the stores for tastings has given me on-air guests I never could have rounded up. Plus, I still love the hot pastrami and cheese!

For a few years, on the advice of a radio consultant, I took on cohosts—two bright women who were different from each other in every way, both of whom inspired my observation that "hosting live radio with a woman is like being married without ever having sex." Or, as I now express it more culinarily: "All of the calories, none of the candy." Yes, it's *that* intimate. And that rife with tensions and resentments. Eventually I went back, quite happily, to flying solo. As scruffy-bearded, no-account men have said in more than a few bad Hollywood movies, "*Baby, I woik alone.*"

The look, feel and reality of for-profit radio (there are other kinds, I know) never stopped changing, led by explosive advances in technology. One moment, there I was in a crowded, tiny studio with racks of cassette tapes covering every wall, with ashtrays for all the smokers and plenty of open countertop for coffee, sodas or beer. Then I blinked and the studio was a sleek, clean, antiseptic cluster of computer monitors, each with color-coded squares and lines tracking like hospital EKGs, at times seeming to edit themselves. Then I blinked again and I was recording segments digitally all over the country and world, on a portable recorder smaller than an old-timer's pack of cigarettes, emailing entire shows to more than one station at a time.

Cooking for charity in Houston; downing street tacos in Cabo San Lucas.

But still…

What matters, I believe, hasn't changed —so I have to ask the question, all these years after backing into a radio career that became the meaning of my professional life: *What matters?*

To me, what matters is the people I've met making radio, the eloquent or not-so-eloquent chefs, winemakers, spirits distillers and beer brewers who share, in our brief moments together, as much of their lives as I can pry out of them while talking with my mouth full. I can remember only a tiny fraction of my guests over this quarter-century. But in a sense, I love them all and am grateful to them all. Together we shared something that was—again, that dangerous word—intimate, and also extraordinary.

We talked to each other over a unique medium in a unique way that, we hoped then as I will hope tomorrow, keeps people from touching that dial. At no time since that fateful lunch at the Sazerac has any part of this felt like my birthright. Like my family before me and now after me, and indeed like life itself, it has been a completely undeserved and never understood free gift.

Inflating a hot-air balloon in Albuquerque; soaking up history and beauty atop the Acropolis in Athens.

APP*e*TIZERS

SMOKED SAUSAGE QUESO

There are few things more Texan than the unrelenting pursuit of molten cheese, and there are few things that taste better in said cheese than smoked sausage. For those who think queso can be made only behind the swinging doors of Tex-Mex restaurants, here's a straightforward process that almost any home cook can navigate.

Ingredients

¾ pound Texas smoked sausage
2 tablespoons olive oil
½ cup finely chopped red onion
½ cup finely chopped green bell pepper
3 cups heavy cream
2 ½ cups shredded Monterey Jack

2 ½ cups shredded Pepper Jack
2 teaspoons cornstarch, dissolved in
 2 teaspoons water
½ cup chopped green onions
Tortilla chips

Serves 10-12

In a food processor, pulse the sausage into a fine crumble. Heat the olive oil in a skillet and brown the sausage over medium-high heat. Add the onion and bell pepper, stirring until caramelized, 4-5 minutes. Add the cream, reduce heat to medium and whisk to incorporate. Gradually add in the cheese, stirring until melted and incorporated. Thicken with the dissolved cornstarch. Garnish with green onion. Serve in a bowl with tortilla chips.

HONEY-JALAPEÑO PARTY DIP

We think the following dip is one of the best treats we know for watching just about any kind of sports on TV. It's spicier than ranch dressing, so it'll encourage you and your guests to imbibe a little bit more. And that makes any contest more fun.

Ingredients

1 cup mayonnaise

⅓ cup thinly sliced green onions

1 ½ teaspoons seeded and minced jalapeños

4 teaspoons honey

¼ teaspoon Worcestershire sauce

¼ teaspoon Tabasco or other hot pepper sauce

⅛ teaspoon black pepper

⅛ teaspoon white pepper

⅛ teaspoon ground red pepper

Serves 6

Whisk the mayonnaise with the remaining ingredients, cover and refrigerate. Serve with tortilla chips.

JALAPEÑO-RED PEPPER HUMMUS

Somehow, all roads must lead to Texas. Otherwise, how can we explain the popularity of this Eastern Mediterranean favorite first encountered in Lebanese or Greek restaurants? Though the basic flavor of ground chick peas, sesame tahini, garlic and lemon is amazing enough, Texas cooks just had to start tinkering to achieve a bit more. With a little kick of heat, naturally.

Ingredients

3 cloves of garlic
1 (15 oz. can chickpeas (garbanzo beans)
⅓ cup tahini
¼ cup lemon juice

½ jalapeño pepper, seeds removed,
   as desired
2 tablespoons extra-virgin olive oil
½ cup roasted red peppers

Serves 8-10

Start by draining and rinsing the chickpeas. Place the garlic cloves in a food processor and pulse a few times. Next add the chickpeas to the food processor, then the tahini. Add the lemon juice, jalapeño and the olive oil. Process the mixture until it's thick and chunky. Now add the roasted red peppers, and process again until the hummus is smooth and creamy. Serve the roasted red pepper hummus with warm pita triangles or pita chips.

CHIPOTLE CHARGRILLED OYSTERS

If there's one thing on earth that's arguably better than New Orleans-style baked oysters—you know, Rockefeller, Bienville and the like—it's their chargrilled next of kin. A dish at chef Hugo Ortega's new Caracol in Houston got me thinking about something like this. And then the flavor of this variation kept me thinking about it long after that.

Ingredients

6 tablespoons butter

3 teaspoons coarsely chopped garlic

3 canned chipotle peppers plus 1 ½ tablespoons adobo
  (liquid reserved from the can)

1 tablespoon chopped parsley

4 cups rock salt

2 dozen Gulf oysters

Serves 6-8

Heat the grill to 450° F. Melt the butter in a small skillet. In a blender, purée the garlic, chipotles, parsley and adobo until smooth. With the blender running, add the butter. Spoon the mixture into a bowl and set aside to cool. Spread the rock salt in the bottom of a pan. Place the oysters, cup-side down, on the rock salt to hold them in place. Roast on the grill until the oysters begin to open, 8 to 10 minutes.

   Remove the hot oysters from the grill and carefully open them, separating the muscle at the top and the bottom and discarding the flat top shell. Spoon about one-half teaspoon of the chipotle butter mixture onto each oyster and then return them to the grill until the butter melts and the oyster plumps and firms, about 3 minutes.

PHYLLO FETA SQUARES

A loose riff on the popular Greek cheese pastry known as tiropita, this recipe mixes feta, cream cheese and eggs to create a smooth filling. Lemon zest adds a welcome accent to the sweet-salty contrast of this appetizer tasted recently on the island of Santorini.

Ingredients

Makes 16 sq.

SAUCE
4 tablespoons unsalted butter
1 tablespoon sugar
8 fresh figs, sliced
½ cup honey

1 pound crumbled feta
1 pound cream cheese
2 large eggs, lightly beaten
¼ cup confectioners sugar
1 teaspoon grated lemon zest
¼ teaspoon salt
12 (17- by 12-inch) phyllo sheets, thawed
  if frozen
1 ¼ sticks unsalted butter, melted then
  cooled slightly
Sesame seeds

To prepare the sauce, melt the butter in a saucepan over medium-low heat and stir in the sugar. Cook and stir just until the sugar has melted and is lightly browned. Remove from heat, and continue stirring until caramelized. Mix in the figs. Over low heat, mix in the honey. Continue to cook and stir 5 minutes, until thickened.

Preheat oven to 400° F with rack in middle. Butter a 13- by-9-inch baking pan. Whisk together feta, cream cheese, eggs, confectioners sugar, zest and salt. Keep stack of phyllo covered with 2 overlapping sheets of plastic wrap. Lay out each dough sheet and brush on butter. Fold in half, brush again, fold in half, cut in half. Place filling on each square of dough. Bring up sides to meet and form a smaller square packet; brush more butter on top. Bake in oven until golden brown and puffed, about 40 minutes. Serve with sauce spooned over top. Sprinkle with sesame seeds.

O nce or twice a year before my mother died, we made the difficult, non-interstate trek from New Orleans to North Louisiana, a world apart from mine. Our destination was Pleasant Hill, a tiny and hardcore Baptist town that always doubted my mother's sanity for marrying a Catholic from New Orleans. If they'd known my Dad was originally from *Boston*, it surely would have been worse.

Happily for all concerned, the winding highway to Pleasant Hill ran straight through Lecompte (pronounced le-COUNT), and Lecompte was home to Lea's Lunchroom. As a child, I always thought it was some kind of miracle that Lea's appeared at the side of the highway beyond its gravel parking lot just in time for lunch. The thought that adults might be able to plan such things had never crossed my mind.

There was always plenty of great country cooking at Lea's, from glazed ham to fried chicken, not to mention fresh-baked pies set out to cool in a kitchen window that had no screen. I ache for the days when things like that still happened, or were legal. Yet without a doubt, the best thing at Lea's was "ole Mr. Lea" himself. Dressed in all manner of white suits and ribbon ties, with a white goatee to complete the look, Lea Johnson was the guy Colonel Sanders looked like when I first became aware of Colonel Sanders.

"Everything tastin' all right for y'all today?" he'd drawl with pure honey in his voice as he stopped by our table. "And you kids. Hmm, I don't see y'all eatin' y'all's vegetables." He'd reach into his pocket and pull out a colorful candy on a stick. "Y'all eat y'all's vegetables and ole Mr. Lea will give y'all a sucka."

That proved it. Ole Mr. Lea was Ole Mr. Lea, even to himself. Of course we ate our vegetables, loving the suckers (known everywhere else as lollipops), craving his candy and his remarkable attention. Who knew that a sucker was the perfect *mignardise* after one or more slices of Lea's Lunchroom pies. My mother always had lemon icebox, the meringue extra high and fluffy, and I (then as now) always went for pecan. I'd bet the place served a great cup of coffee, but I didn't take up *that* uncontrollable love until freshman year of college, when I learned that a Southern boy's ice-cold Coke didn't help when the temperature dropped 30 degrees during a Boston University football game.

I know, I know…you *can't* go home again. And after my mother died, perhaps bearing a sadness I can understand only now, my father took us back to Pleasant Hill only once. Eventually sadness and loneliness compelled him to remarry, to another woman who would die before he did, and Pleasant Hill faded even farther into the distance and the mists. Yet I *did* manage to go home again, to Pleasant Hill and eventually to Lea's Lunchroom.

At BU, in a class about Anton Chekhov, the Russian-accented professor said that instead of a term paper we could write a short story in the style of Chekhov. The thought of mimicking one of my literary heroes felt weird, even to a college freshman with little more than a clue—yet the story I titled "In the Country" was the result. It was all there from that final visit: the awkward conversations among two grandparents who'd lost their daughter, a husband who'd lost his wife and children who'd lost their mother, those current and remembered walks out from the wooden porch to the crumbling stone wall beneath the magnolias, and the searing memory of my mother collecting fireflies in a jar so they could deliver light whenever I got scared after dark in a very strange place.

Lea's came into my life twice after that, though I'd be totally happy if it did so again. I was asked to write about it once, though only long distance, for *Louisiana Life* magazine. And then, on a business trip to some new casino with my oldest daughter, we stopped at Lea's in Lecompte because…I said we had to. Lea and his wife Georgie were long gone, of course, and their daughter Ann had moved back from Houston to run the place. Before long, she and I were taping an entirely unplanned *Delicious Mischief,* both of us remembering her father.

I've been eating, and every so often loving, my vegetables ever since. Yet ole Mr. Lea remains the only one who ever gave me a sucka for doing so.

GRILLED SHRIMP REMOULADE

In New Orleans, shrimp remoulade is a favorite appetizer in many restaurants, plain and fancy. But nowhere more than at Arnaud's in the French Quarter, which calls its version Shrimp Arnaud and even bottles the dressing commercially. Arnaud's was the subject of my second cookbook, forcing me to dine there two or even three times a week for three years, with the late great European-trained proprietor Archie Casbarian. I can't tell you how much I learned about food and wine (and Armagnac!) from Archie, whose kids run Arnaud's now. The fact that I still love this very different spin on remoulade, though not Arnaud's secret recipe, is my tribute and a toast to him.

2 pounds jumbo shrimp, peeled
¼ cup vegetable oil
2 tablespoons freshly squeezed lemon juice
3 cloves garlic, chopped
1 teaspoon salt
Romaine lettuce leaves

REMOULADE
2 tablespoons Creole mustard
1 tablespoon red wine vinegar
Salt and black pepper to taste
1 cup olive oil
1 tablespoon paprika
½ cup diced celery
1 cup diced green onions

1 teaspoon minced garlic
½ cup finely chopped parsley
2 tablespoons freshly grated horseradish
⅛ teaspoon ground red pepper
2 tablespoons lemon juice

Ingredients

Serves 8

Place the shrimp in a glass bowl with the oil, lemon juice, garlic and salt, mixing to coat thoroughly. Cover and set the bowl in the refrigerator to marinate for 3 hours. Prepare the remoulade by whisking together the mustard with the vinegar in a mixing bowl. Season to taste with salt and pepper. Gradually add the olive oil, whisking constantly, followed by all remaining remoulade ingredients. When ready to serve, grill the shrimp over hot coals for 5-7 minutes, turning halfway through. Set shrimp on plates atop lettuce leaves and spoon remoulade over the top and sides.

SALMON TARTARE *with* MEXICAN AVOCADOS

Salmon isn't particularly a Texas fish, except that millions of Texans love it. Much of it hails from the Pacific Northwest—which, according to my biased Texas taste buds, means it can use all the flavor help it can get. This combination of salmon and avocados from south of the border is almost as good to look at as it is to eat.

Ingredients

1 pound fresh salmon, finely minced
1 red onion, peeled and finely diced
3 ounces finely cut chives
Juice of 3 lemons
2 tablespoons extra-virgin olive oil
2 avocados
½ cup of buttermilk

Salt and white pepper
4 large shallots
2 tablespoons brown sugar
½ cup rice wine vinegar
1 English cucumber, thinly shaved
1 head frisse lettuce

Serves 4

Mix salmon, onions and chives together in a bowl and keep refrigerated. Mix ½ of the lemon juice and olive oil together and season with salt and pepper to make a dressing. Purée avocados with buttermilk, remainder of lemon juice and salt and pepper. Slice shallots into rings. Mix sugar and vinegar together and bring to boil. Add sliced shallots and let cool. Combine the salmon mixture with the dressing. Place a large spoonful of avocado mix on plate. Carefully place salmon mix in the center of avocado mix. In a separate bowl, mix frisee with cucumbers and pickled shallots. Garnish salmon with salad.

PAN-ASIAN BBQ OYSTERS

There's nothing particularly "New Orleans" about these Asian-tasting oysters, except maybe that they start out as oysters on the half shell and end up baked. Still, there's nothing Rockefeller or Bienville going on top of them either. I first tasted this recipe a year ago at a wonderful New Orleans place called Mike's on the Avenue—and friends have been asking me how to make "those great oysters from Mike's" ever since. I wangled this recipe from Chef Mike himself for some cookbook or other.

Ingredients

Serves 8

2 tablespoons tomato paste

2 garlic cloves

2 shallots

2 teaspoons minced red onion

2 teaspoons minced cilantro

½ teaspoon toasted Szechuan peppercorns
 (or crushed red pepper)

2 teaspoons minced mild chile pepper

2 ½ tablespoons white vinegar

⅓ cup firmly packed brown sugar

⅓ cup sesame oil

4 teaspoons grated fresh ginger

½ teaspoon ground red (cayenne) pepper

Juice of 1 ½ lemons

½ cup teriyaki sauce

⅓ cup soy sauce

3 dashes Tabasco or other hot pepper sauce

½ pound pancetta (or bacon)

2 dozen oysters on the half shell

Blend all ingredients except pancetta and oysters in a food processor. Roast the pancetta in the oven until lightly browned. Pat dry and crumble or finely chop. Prepare fire in a grill. Place the oysters on the half shell directly above the coals and top with the sauce. Sprinkle with pancetta. Grill until oysters are bubbly, 5-7 minutes.

RASPBERRY CHIPOTLE BBQ MEATBALLS

Nearly a decade before we decided I should write their cookbook, I was impressed by Case Fischer and Wieser—especially by the salsas, sauces and marinades they put out from Fischer & Wieser Specialty Foods in Fredericksburg. The guys have been on my radio show many times, inspiring one of my most popular dishes. It's made with their first great sauce that attracted national and even international attention. If only it had taught all the waiters on earth how to pronounce chi-POTE-lay.

Ingredients

Serves 6

2 pounds lean ground beef
1 cup dry breadcrumbs
⅔ cup finely chopped onion
½ cup milk
2 tablespoons chopped fresh parsley
2 teaspoons salt
1 teaspoon Worcestershire sauce
⅛ teaspoon black pepper

2 eggs
1 ½ cups Fischer & Wieser's The Original Roasted Raspberry Chipotle Sauce
1 ½ cups prepared barbecue sauce
3 tablespoons prepared ketchup
2 tablespoons prepared yellow mustard
2 tablespoons cider vinegar

Heat oven to 400° F. In a large mixing bowl, combine beef, breadcrumbs, onion, milk, parsley, salt, Worcestershire, pepper and eggs. Shape into small (1-inch) meatballs. Place in ungreased rectangular pan, or on rack in broiler pan. Bake uncovered about 20 minutes, until no longer pink in center and juice is clear. While meatballs are cooking, prepare the sauce, in a pan large enough to also hold the meatballs, over medium heat. Combine all remaining ingredients and bring to a boil, then reduce heat and let simmer. When meatballs are cooked, drain them of fat and transfer them to the sauce, letting them simmer for 30 minutes. Serve hot in a chafing dish with toothpicks.

LAMB MEATBALLS *with* MINT TOMATO SAUCE

For me, lamb and mint go together not so much because of the roast lamb with mint jelly served all over the British Isles but because of the thousand (much more flavorful) variations I've tasted in places like Greece, Turkey, Israel and Lebanon. I'd have to say, there's a lot more Beirut than Brighton in this recipe for cocktail meatballs.

Ingredients

Serves 6-8

2 pounds ground lamb
3 tablespoons chopped blanched almonds
4 tablespoons dried bread crumbs
4 tablespoons chopped fresh mint
1 tablespoon chopped fresh parsley
3 cloves garlic, minced
1 egg, lightly beaten
2 teaspoons ground cumin
1 ½ teaspoon Creole seasoning

1 teaspoon lemon pepper
½ teaspoon crushed red pepper
¼ teaspoon black pepper
4 tablespoons olive oil
1 onion, finely chopped
2 cups crushed tomatoes in
    thick purée
½ cup chicken broth
¼ cup dry white wine

In a medium bowl, combine the lamb, almonds, bread crumbs, 2 tablespoons of the mint, half the parsley, the egg, garlic, 1 teaspoon of the cumin, 1 teaspoon of the Creole seasoning, lemon pepper, crushed red pepper and black pepper. Shape the mixture into about 30 small meatballs. In a large nonstick frying pan, heat 2 tablespoons of the oil over moderately high heat. Add the meatballs and cook, turning, until browned all over, about 3 minutes. Drain on paper towels.

In a large deep frying pan, heat the remaining 2 tablespoons of oil over medium-low heat. Add the onion and cook, stirring occasionally, until translucent, about 5 minutes. Add the tomatoes, broth, white wine, the remaining 1 teaspoon cumin and ½ teaspoon Creole seasoning. Bring to a simmer, reduce the heat and simmer, covered, for 10 minutes. Add the meatballs to the tomato sauce and simmer, covered, until the meatballs are cooked through, about 10 minutes longer. Stir in the remaining mint and parsley.

UMBRIAN TRUFFLED ARTICHOKE FLAN

Whenever the weather turns a bit cooler in Texas, I think back to the wonderful foods I tasted in the Italian region of Umbria—most familiar for St. Francis of Assisi, but increasingly recognized for its wines, produce and cured meats. I think this recipe is a fascinating and unexpected use for the truffles that hail from the region's lovely hillsides.

Ingredients

Serves 6

FOR THE FLAN

Extra-virgin olive oil to coat the molds
Bread crumbs to coat the molds
¾ pound artichokes
2 tablespoons lemon juice
½ cup vegetable broth
2 tablespoons freshly grated Parmigiano Reggiano
2 large eggs, beaten to blend
⅓ cup plus 1 tablespoon heavy cream
¼ teaspoon salt
⅛ teaspoon freshly ground black pepper

FOR THE SAUCE

3 tablespoons unsalted butter
¼ cup unbleached all-purpose flour
2 cups whole milk, heated to boiling
¼ teaspoon salt
⅛ teaspoon freshly ground black pepper
2 tablespoons grated fresh black truffle

Make the flan: Preheat the oven to 350° F. Coat 6 individual (1-cup) soufflé molds with olive oil and bread crumbs. Refrigerate. Trim the artichokes; immediately place in cool water with the lemon juice to prevent oxidation. Drain and slice the artichokes, and place in a pan with the broth. Cook until very tender over medium heat. Purée the sautéed artichokes until smooth in a food processor. Place in a bowl and add the Parmigiano, eggs, cream, salt and pepper. Fill the prepared molds with the mixture and place in a roasting pan filled halfway with warm water. Bake in the preheated oven 25 minutes, or until set.

Meanwhile, make the sauce: Melt the butter in a small pan. Add the flour and cook over low heat, whisking all the time, for 2 minutes, or until the flour loses its raw smell. Do not let the flour take on any color. Slowly add the warm milk, whisking all the while to avoid lumps. Season with the salt and pepper and cook until thick, whisking often, about 10 minutes after it reaches a boil. Whisk in the grated truffle and keep warm. Spoon the sauce onto 6 plates. Place a flan on each plate and serve hot.

TAPAS TORTILLAS

I love Spanish tortillas—those wonderful omelet-meets-frittata things so popular in every corner of Spain, without so much as an actual Mexican tortilla in sight. Some years ago, I started playing around with transforming classic "tortilla Espanola" into a finger food for parties at my house. It transforms quite well, thank you. And they're equally great for brunch or breakfast as well.

6 eggs
2 tablespoons half-and-half
 (or cream or milk)
½ teaspoon salt
¼ teaspoon ground black pepper
1 pinch powdered saffron
1 tablespoon olive oil

1 tablespoon butter
1 cup coarsely chopped fresh mushrooms
2 cloves garlic, minced
2 cups frozen loose-pack diced hash brown
 potatoes with onions and peppers
¼ cup snipped fresh chives

Preheat oven to 450° F. Grease an 8x8x2-inch baking pan; set aside. In a medium bowl, whisk together eggs, half-and-half, cream or milk, salt, pepper and saffron. Set aside. In a large skillet, heat olive oil and butter over medium heat until butter is melted. Add mushrooms and garlic, cook for 1 minute. Stir in potatoes. Cover and cook over medium-low heat about 10 minutes or until potatoes are lightly browned and tender, stirring occasionally. Remove from heat, stir in chives.

Spread potato mixture evenly into prepared baking pan. Pour egg mixture evenly over potato mixture, pressing down lightly with the back of a spoon to completely cover potatoes. Bake, uncovered, about 15 minutes or until set and top is golden (center may puff during baking, but will fall during standing time). Remove from oven, let stand 5 minutes. Cut into 1-inch squares. Serve warm.

BRISKET-STUFFED 1015 ONIONS

Everybody in Texas loves smoked beef brisket, and everybody in Texas loves the sweet onions developed by Texas A&M and known in the marketplace as 1015s. We wondered how good it might be if we found a way to stuff one inside the other. Turns out, we're pretty excited about the result.

Ingredients

10 large Texas 1015 onions
1 pound smoked beef brisket, shredded
½ teaspoon minced garlic
1 teaspoon sage
½ teaspoon ground red pepper

½ teaspoon cumin
½ teaspoon salt
½ teaspoon black pepper
1 cup unseasoned bread crumbs

Serves 10

Peel the onions and boil in salted water about 10 minutes, then drain reserving the water. Cut the centers from the onions to create shells. Heat the shredded brisket in a sauté pan, adding the garlic and seasonings. Stir over medium heat about 2 minutes. Remove from heat and stir in the bread crumbs. Spoon the brisket stuffing into the onions and set in a shallow baking dish. Add enough of the reserved onion water to cover the bottom of the dish. Bake in a preheated 350° F oven until onions are tender, about 45 minutes.

OPEN-FACED HOT MUFFALETTA

In New Orleans, I'm convinced the essence of muffaletta sandwich goodness is not found in the meats or the cheeses but in the olive salad. So it's only right that the greater portion of this recipe is devoted to that.

Makes 16 — *Ingredients*

OLIVE SALAD

1 cup coarsely chopped, pitted, large green Greek olives

1 cup coarsely chopped queen size Manzanilla olives with pimentos

1 (15.5 ounce) jar Italian giardiniera vegetables, chopped

1 tablespoon minced fresh parsley

1 tablespoon minced garlic

2 teaspoons capers, drained and rinsed

½ teaspoon dried oregano

½ cup plus 1 tablespoon extra-virgin olive oil

⅛ teaspoon salt

⅛ teaspoon black pepper

⅛ teaspoon white pepper

⅛ teaspoon crushed red pepper flakes

1 15-inch loaf French bread

¼ pound sliced Genoa salami

¾ pound sliced provolone cheese

¼ pound sliced baked ham

¼ pound sliced mortadella

Prepare the olive salad by combining all ingredients in a large bowl. Cover and let marinate in the refrigerator for at least 4 hours before using. Slice French bread in half lengthwise. Lay open halves on a baking sheet and spread the tops with most of the olive salad. Divide the salami over the sandwiches, followed by half the cheese, the ham and the mortadella. Top with the remaining provolone. Drizzle with a bit of olive oil from the Olive Salad, if desired. Bake in a preheated 350º F oven for about 10 minutes, until the cheese is melted, then broil for 2-3 minutes to turn the top golden brown. Slice each open-faced sandwich into 8 pieces and serve with the remaining olive salad as garnish.

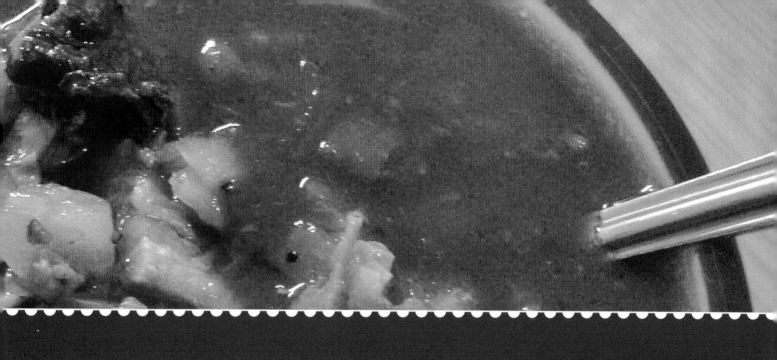

SOUPS

GUMBO NIGHT *in* MARFA

A few summers back, before I bought my house in Marfa—that oh-so-artsy enclave in Far West Texas—I took up housesitting in a big country place on the northwest side of town, with a backyard garden bursting with tomatoes, squash and cantaloupe and a black-and-white border collie named Al that I was supposed to walk over the hills once or twice a day. With no TV and no phone, I cooked and ate out of this garden all week—tomatoes in everything, of course, and demand still couldn't keep up with supply. One night I even overpowered an 18-inch-long zucchini enough to whip up a Moroccan version of couscous, complete with chick peas, pine nuts and sultanas—and cocktail-sized meatballs, just because I wanted them. And then, with company coming from my hometown of New Orleans by way of Fort Davis up the road in Jeff Davis County, it suddenly was Gumbo Night in Marfa. I'm not sure the town has been the same since.

1 whole chicken, 4-5 pounds	Garlic powder
3 yellow onions	Onion powder
3 stalks celery	Powdered caldo de pollo, optional
1-2 pounds andouille or other smoked sausage, sliced	1 cup all-purpose flour
	1 cup vegetable oil
2 green bell peppers	Tabasco or other hot pepper sauce
1 pound fresh (or frozen) okra	Steamed white rice
2 cups tomato salsa (controversial, see Note below)	Chopped green onions
Creole seasoning to taste	
Black pepper	

Ingredients

Serves 6-30

To make the stock (while cleverly cooking the chicken), cut up the whole chicken and set in a large stockpot, filling with water. Sacrifice 1 onion and 1 stalk celery, chopping and adding to the water—along with scraps from all other vegetables cut up a bit later. Season with Creole seasoning and bring almost to a boil, reduce heat. Simmer for about 1 hour, until the chicken is cooked. Remove chicken and let cool enough to handle.

While stock is being made, heat some oil in a large (preferably cast iron) pot, kettle or Dutch oven. Brown the sausage pieces until starting to get crisp on outside, then chop and add—2 remaining onions, 2 remaining stalks celery, 2 bell peppers. Stir until the onion starts to caramelize—don't be afraid of golden brown, for here lies flavor. Stir in cut-up okra and cook until the "strings" of sticky stuff begin to cook out—don't be afraid of sticky stuff, for here lies thickening (not to mention the West African name for okra that gives us "gumbo.")

Add the salsa, or other chopped or purée tomato—RO*TEL is great for this, too. Season the thick, vegetal mixture with Creole seasoning and all other spices. Strain the stock into the gumbo pot. Taste and add caldo de pollo powder (chicken bouillon) for a more intense chicken flavor. Debone the chicken and add the meat in bite-sized chunks. In a separate pan or skillet, thoroughly combine the flour and oil until smooth, cooking over medium-heat until this roux turns dark brown. And no, don't be afraid of heat—just, as the old saying goes, *watch that basket!* To help smoothly incorporate the roux into the gumbo, carefully pour a cup of the gumbo into the roux in the skillet—DO be afraid of a steam burn to your hands. Get in, and get out fast. Stir the roux, applying more gumbo until it's a kind of delicious-smelling sludge. This is perfect to add to gumbo.

Add roux and let gumbo simmer another hour or so, so all the ingredients can learn to get along. Season again as needed. Add pepper sauce as desired. When ready to serve, ladle gumbo over steamed white rice in large bowls, topping with chopped green onions. Serves, well, 6-30, depending.

NOTE: In southwest Louisiana, the heart of Cajun Country, putting any kind of tomato in gumbo is heresy. In New Orleans, the heart of Creole country, putting tomato in gumbo is almost mandatory. I love the burnt sienna color and the extra layer of complex sweetness tomato brings—and I haven't worked on cookbooks with bazillions of great chefs over the years not to care about layers! I've tried all versions of tomato in gumbo and, by far, the best, is chunky tomato salsa right from the supermarket. Don't yell, don't scream—just eat it, okay? Which, I promise, even if you're from gray-gumbo Lafayette, you WILL!

CHICKEN TORTILLA SOUP

Every so often, I simply need a "tortilla soup fix." It's something that happens to people when they move to Texas and, best I can tell, the condition never goes away. For some folks, a tortilla soup craving requires a visit to a favorite Mexican or Tex-Mex restaurant. For me, once I discovered this simple recipe, not so much.

Ingredients

Serves 8-10

2 yellow onions, chopped
2 large carrots, finely chopped
2 tablespoons olive oil
1 tablespoon minced garlic
1 roasted chicken, bones and skin removed, meat cut into bite-sized pieces
8 cups chicken broth
2 cups chunky tomato salsa
½ cup freshly squeezed lime juice, plus additional

¼ cup plus ¼ cup chopped cilantro leaves
1 tablespoon chopped jalapeno, or to taste
½ teaspoon garlic powder
½ teaspoon onion powder
Salt and black pepper to taste
1 tomato, chopped
2 avocados, chopped
½ cup grated cheddar or jack cheese

Sauté the onion and carrot until they begin to caramelize, then add the garlic for a couple of quick stirs, just enough to release its flavor. Stir in the chunks of chicken, combining. Add the chicken broth, followed by the salsa and lime juice. Bring to a quick boil, then reduce heat to a simmer. Add the chopped cilantro and season with jalapeno, garlic and onion powders, and salt and pepper. Simmer for about 30 minutes so flavors can meld. When ready to serve, ladle the soup into large bowls and garnish with remaining cilantro, tomato, avocado and cheese. Splash with additional lime juice, if desired.

FLORIDA STONE CRAB SOUP

I tasted my life's first soup made with delicious Florida stone crabs at Miller's Oyster House in Everglades City south of Naples, on the edge of the vast wetlands national park of that name. Restaurant owner Bobby Miller insisted he'd never written down the real recipe for this soup, beloved during the annual October 15-May 15 stone crab season, but he was happy enough to rattle off ingredients. The basic underpinning is tomato-based Manhattan clam chowder, minus the clams and clam juice, of course. The wine, as usual, is my idea.

Ingredients
Serves 8-10

3 tablespoons extra-virgin olive oil
2 carrots, peeled and sliced
1 green bell pepper, chopped
2 celery stalks, chopped
1 onion, chopped
1 large garlic clove, minced
¼ cup dry white wine
½ teaspoon dried thyme
¼ teaspoon dried rosemary
2 bay leaves

1 cup tomato juice (or V8, or Bloody Mary
   mix for extra kick)
1 cup canned peeled tomatoes
½ cup canned crushed tomatoes
1 pound potatoes, peeled and cut into
   2-inch chunks
1 pound Florida stone crab meat,
   cut in chunks
Tabasco or other pepper hot sauce
Salt and black pepper to taste

Heat the olive oil in a large pot or kettle and sauté the carrots, bell pepper, celery and onion until soft and translucent, about 5 minutes. Add the garlic and cook for another minute. Add the white wine and stir until it evaporates. Add the herbs and tomato products, then the potato chunks. Cover and simmer gently until the potatoes are tender, 30-40 minutes. Only then add the stone crab meat, which will shred and incorporate into the soup. Add the Tabasco. Season to taste with salt and black pepper. Remove the bay leaves. Serve hot in bowls.

MY DATE WITH JULIA CHILD

It took six weeks of planning, plus the purchase of an air ticket and the reservation of a hotel room, for me to stand at a certain front door in a posh oceanfront development outside Santa Barbara—and *knock*. I'd already had to talk my way past a guard for the gated community, but the biggest challenge to my occasionally persuasive gift of gab was still to come.

"Oh hull-oo," said the familiar voice from somewhere above my head. It was a friendly voice, but non-committal, you might say "professionally friendly." Indeed, I did let my eyes wander north a bit, until they found the face that launched a thousand PBS telethons. Julia Child was standing at that door, in a simple, casual pantsuit, with little or possibly no makeup, and her hair barely brushed to face the morning.

The time was the mid-1980s, and I was food editor of *United Press International*. I'd traveled cross-country at considerable expense (*UPI*'s) to interview Julia, as everyone called her from the start, for an extensive feature in a series known as Lifesize. God only knows how many publicists had put their heads together on this one. But in the end, it was only me standing at the door, babbling something that included my name, my affiliation and my appointment day and time.

"I'm so very sorry," Julia said. "I suppose this was all set up correctly, but I had to have knee surgery yesterday. And as you can imagine, I don't quite feel my best today. I think you'd be much happier with our interview if you came back another day."

A thousand angry faces flashed through my mind, all of them belonging to the feature editor of *UPI,* a woman not known for compassion or even sanity. I babbled a bit more, I don't recall what: about flying to Los Angeles from New Orleans and driving up to Santa Barbara in a rental car, about—well, by this point, I suspect I was begging.

Finally, Julia said, "Well, all right. In that case, let's just see what we can do, shall we?"

For the next seven to eight hours, sitting on the couch, peeking around the house or settling at the table for a light lunch—all with Julia's husband Paul in remarkable attendance, saying little but *belonging* to everything—I got to relive Julia Child's incredible life. I heard about her mother who couldn't boil water, about her romantic meeting with Paul in war-torn China, about her food epiphany in post-war France. I got her take on the years of struggle toward the cookbook that became *Mastering the Art of French Cooking*, and the primitive TV series in Boston that became *The French Chef*.

And when I asked if she had any regrets, I caught her eyes seeking Paul's across the room. "Only, you know," and she paused, as though the words caught in her throat. "Only that we never had any children," she said, and Paul nodded. As I was just about to turn the notebook page, Julia picked up the thought again. "But, many people—many young women, especially—have told me they've found a career, found a life really, because of the things that I've done." She giggled. "Of course, I can't imagine *why*. But sometimes, I think of all those people as our children."

CHILLED TOMATO & PEANUT SOUP

This might at first seem an odd choice for a soup, but then again, a lot of folks think chilled soups are odd anyway. Still, in the summer, when even reluctant fancies turn to Spanish gazpacho or French vichyssoise, you should consider this intriguing and delicious combination of flavors.

Ingredients

2 tablespoons olive oil
1 cup finely chopped onion
2 tablespoons all-purpose flour
3 cups whole milk

½ cup smooth peanut butter
1 teaspoon celery salt
Freshly ground black pepper to taste
3 cups tomato juice

Serves 6

Heat the oil and sauté the onions until softened but not brown, then stir in the flour and cook for 2 minutes. Remove the pot from heat. In a bowl, stir the milk gradually into the peanut butter until the mixture is smooth, then add the celery salt and pepper. Add this slowly to the onion mixture. Return the pan to the heat and simmer, stirring often, until soup thickens. Stir in the tomato juice. Refrigerate at least 1 hour before serving in a tureen or in individual soup bowls.

CHILLED CHUNKY GAZPACHO

When the summer here in Texas seems to grind on forever, I always do what the Spaniards around Valencia taught me to do on my very first visit three decades ago—whip up a chilled soup full of great nutrition and bright flavors. These days, when so many odd things turn up in cold soups called gazpacho, it sure is a joy to have them not.

Ingredients

Serves 4-6

5 large Roma tomatoes, diced
1 (15.5 ounce) can garbanzo beans, drained and rinsed
1 stalk celery, diced
1 cucumber—peeled, seeded and diced
2 green onions, chopped
2 tablespoons finely chopped sweet onion
¼ cup chopped fresh parsley
½ red bell pepper, diced
½ yellow bell pepper, diced
½ lemon, juiced
1 clove garlic, minced
1 (46-ounce) can tomato juice
1 teaspoon curry powder
1 pinch of dried tarragon
Freshly ground black pepper to taste
1 dash Tabasco or other hot pepper sauce

In a large glass bowl, mix the tomatoes, garbanzo beans, celery, cucumber, green onions, sweet onion, parsley, red bell pepper, yellow bell pepper, lemon juice and garlic. Pour in the tomato juice. Season with curry powder, tarragon, pepper and hot pepper sauce. Chill in the refrigerator at least 2 hours before serving.

CHILLED TEXAS WATERMELON SOUP

On an overheated late summer afternoon, when even the blacktop of our Texas country roads seems to be melting, there are few things better than the bright red insides of a local watermelon. Unless maybe it's this chilled watermelon soup, given extra zing by fresh mint and ginger, plus just a touch of saltiness by a crumble of feta cheese.

Ingredients

6 pounds yellow or red seedless Texas watermelon, diced (9 cups)

2 tablespoons chopped fresh mint

1 tablespoon sugar

2 tablespoons fresh lemon juice

1 cup lightly sweet white wine (such as Riesling)

1 teaspoon finely chopped ginger

8 teaspoons crumbled feta

¼ cup sparkling wine (or sparkling water)

Serves 8

Combine 1 cup of the watermelon with mint and sugar in a bowl. Blend remaining 8 cups watermelon, lemon juice, wine and ginger in a blender until smooth. Let it sit for half an hour. Strain soup; divide among 8 bowls. Top each with ⅛ cup reserved watermelon and 1 teaspoon feta.

HOT & SOUR SOUP

I hate to break this news to you, but Paul Prudhomme is not Chinese. Still, the other night I prepared Chinese hot and sour soup using as many lessons as I could remember from Chef Paul years ago in New Orleans. Why use one kind of pepper, he'd ask, when it's better to use several? Why use one form of garlic, he'd ask, when it's better to use several? The result is more and better flavors that stroke different taste buds on a different schedule. In fact, that's always the result when we let the Cajun master power how we think about and make our food.

Ingredients

Serves 6

¼ pound pork tenderloin or chop, sliced into thin 1-inch boneless strips
1 teaspoon dry sherry
2 tablespoons soy sauce
2 tablespoons dried black cloud/wood's ear mushrooms
1 tablespoon extra-virgin olive oil
2 tablespoons finely chopped onion
1 tablespoon minced garlic

½ teaspoon onion powder
½ teaspoon garlic powder
1 teaspoon finely chopped fresh ginger root
1 teaspoon crushed red pepper
1 teaspoon sriracha chile garlic paste (more if desired)
1 cup Asian mushrooms, such as straw or shiitake, or mixed
½ cup sliced bamboo shoots
1 quart chicken broth

1 square firm tofu, cut into strips
2 teaspoons sesame oil
2 tablespoons white vinegar
2 tablespoons seasoned rice vinegar
2 teaspoons cornstarch, dissolved in water
1 egg, beaten
Chopped green onions

Marinate the pork in sherry and 1 tablespoon soy sauce for about 30 minutes. Combine dried mushrooms in a bowl with water to rehydrate, then drain and slice. Heat the oil in a large pan or pot and stir-fry the strips till lightly browned. Stir in onion, garlic, ginger, onion and garlic powders, crushed red pepper and sriracha. Add the two kinds of mushrooms to heat through, along with the bamboo shoots. Pour in the broth, followed by the tofu, sesame oil, 1 tablespoon soy sauce and the vinegars. Add more vinegar if desired. Bring to a low boil and add the cornstarch, bubbling until soup thickens. Add beaten egg, stirring gently once. Remove from heat. Sprinkle with chopped green onions and serve.

HARVEST CHICKEN CHOWDER

As the weather turns cool and it's autumn across Texas (even when the days heat up now and again), it's hard to think of anything better than this thickened, vegetable-laden version of chicken soup. And this being Texas, it arrives with no small amount of cheddar cheese.

Ingredients

Serves 6-8

2 cups shredded sharp Cheddar cheese
2 tablespoons olive oil
1 cup diced onion
1 cup diced celery
8 to 12 ounces diced chicken apple sausage
1 cup apple cider
2 ½ cups chicken broth
1 cup diced carrot

2 cups diced potato
1 cup diced cooked chicken
1 cup corn kernels
2 ½ cups milk
½ cup all-purpose flour
1 tablespoon fresh chopped parsley,
   or 1 teaspoon dried parsley flakes
Salt and pepper to taste

Heat olive oil in a large saucepan or Dutch oven; add chopped onion, celery and diced sausage. Cook over medium heat, stirring, until onion and celery are wilted and sausage is lightly browned. Add the apple cider, chicken broth, carrots and potatoes. Bring to a boil over high heat. Reduce heat to medium-low and cover; simmer for 30 minutes, or until vegetables are tender. Add the corn and chicken. In a medium bowl, whisk 1 cup of the milk with the ½ cup of flour. Stir into the pot with the remaining 1 ½ cups of milk. Cook, stirring, until thickened. Stir in cheese until melted and the chowder is hot. Add parsley and salt and pepper, to taste.

ROASTED CAULIFLOWER SOUP

This dish is another of my love poems to caramelization, the cooking process that turns boring into beautiful. If there's one thing professional chefs do that home cooks are afraid to do, it's caramelize everything that doesn't caramelize them first. Who knew that "golden brown" was a flavor every bit as much as it is a color.

2 heads cauliflower
3 garlic cloves
2 shallots
2 tablespoons olive oil
3 cups chicken broth

1 cup water
1 teaspoon finely chopped fresh thyme leaves
1 bay leaf
2 cups heavy cream

Ingredients

Serves 6-8

Preheat oven to 425° F. Cut cauliflower into 1-inch flowerets (about 10 cups). In a large baking pan toss cauliflower, garlic and shallots with oil to coat and roast in middle of oven about 30 minutes, or until golden brown. In a 4-quart kettle simmer broth, water, roasted cauliflower mixture and herbs 30 minutes, or until cauliflower is very tender. Discard bay leaf and in a blender purée soup in batches until smooth (use caution when blending hot liquids), transferring to a bowl. Return soup to kettle and stir in cream and salt and pepper to taste. Heat soup over moderate heat until just heated through.

CREAM *of* PUMPKIN SOUP

As we in Texas head slowly into the fall and start seeing pumpkins everywhere we turn, it's nice to remember that these things were foods before they were Halloween decorations. This lush soup topped with grilled Gulf shrimp has always been one of my favorite pumpkin recipes.

Ingredients

Serves 6

1 ½ pounds fresh pumpkin, cut in chunks and roasted 1 hour at 350° F
2 quarts chicken broth
1 quart heavy cream
10 fresh sage leaves
½ tablespoons chopped fresh thyme

1 tablespoon diced shallots
4 cloves fresh garlic
4 tablespoons honey
Salt and black pepper to taste
6 large shrimp

Bring the pumpkin to a boil in the chicken broth and cream, adding all remaining ingredients except shrimp. When pumpkin is tender, remove from the heat and let cool enough to handle. Pour the soup into a food processor and purée until smooth. Strain through a sieve. Return the soup to heat. Grill the shrimp, or sear them in a very hot skillet. To serve, ladle the hot soup into a bowl. Set a shrimp at the center of each bowl.

THAI TOM YUM GOONG

Yes, it's too damned hot in Texas. But it's also too damned hot in Thailand. That doesn't keep cooks there from making one of the world's most famous hot soups. It's clearly based on the principle of all Southern cultures: that making you sweat actually cools you down.

Ingredients

Serves 4

6 cups good-quality chicken stock

4 kaffir lime leaves
   (can be purchased frozen)

2 stalks minced lemongrass, or 3 tablespoon frozen prepared lemongrass

2 teaspoons minced garlic

1 fresh red chili, minced, or ½ to ¾ teaspoon dried crushed chili

1 cup sliced fresh shiitake mushrooms

¼ cup lime juice

3 tablespoons fish sauce

8-12 medium to large shrimp, fresh or frozen, shells removed

½ cup fresh cilantro

1 tablespoon chopped fresh basil

Coconut milk if needed

Thai Nam Prik Pao chili sauce—if desired

Place stock in a large pot over high heat. Add the minced lemongrass (and leftover lemongrass stalks, if using fresh), plus kaffir lime leaves. Bring to a boil. When soup reaches a bubbling boil, turn heat down to medium. Add the garlic, chili, mushrooms, lime juice and fish sauce. Stir well. Partially cover with a lid and simmer 3 minutes. Add the shrimp, gently stirring them in. Simmer until shrimp are pink and plump (2-3 minutes). Remove soup from heat and do a taste-test, looking for a balance of salty, sour and spicy. If the soup needs more salt, add 1 tablespoon more fish sauce. If it's too sour, add a little brown sugar. If too spicy (Tom Yum is meant to be spicy!), add a little coconut milk. If too salty, add another squeeze of lime juice.

As a final touch, add a dollop or two of Thai Nam Prik Pao chili sauce. The sauce will turn the soup a little red in color, but will bring the flavor up to a whole new level. It can also be served on the side in small dishes, so guests can add as much as they prefer. Ladle the soup into bowls and top with a generous sprinkling of cilantro and basil.

AUTHENTIC VIETNAMESE PHO

Texas in general, and Houston in particular, have large Vietnamese populations, many of whom opened restaurants as their first rung up the American ladder. I learned to love pho from totally non-Asian chefs, one British and one Australian, who took me for this substantial beef soup after they got off work around midnight. It's good other times, too.

Ingredients

Serves 6

5 pounds beef knuckle, with meat
2 pounds beef oxtail
1 white (daikon) radish, sliced
2 onions, chopped
2 ounces whole star anise pods
½ cinnamon stick
2 whole cloves
1 teaspoon black peppercorns
1 slice fresh ginger root
1 tablespoon white sugar
1 tablespoon salt
1 tablespoon fish sauce
1 ½ pounds dried flat rice noodles
½ pound frozen beef sirloin

TOPPINGS

Sriracha hot pepper sauce
Hoisin sauce
Thinly sliced onion
Chopped fresh cilantro
Bean sprouts (mung beans)
Thai sweet basil
Thinly sliced green onion
Limes, quartered

Place the beef knuckle in a very large (9 quart or more) pot. Season with salt, and fill pot with 2 gallons of water. Bring to a boil, and cook for about 2 hours. Skim fat from the surface of the soup, and add the oxtail, radish and onions. Tie the anise pods, cinnamon stick, cloves, peppercorns and ginger in a cheesecloth or place in a spice bag; add to the soup. Stir in sugar, salt and fish sauce. Simmer over medium-low heat for at least 4 more hours (the longer, the better).

At the end of cooking, taste, and add salt as needed. Strain broth, and return to the pot to keep at a simmer. Discard spices and bones. Reserve meat from the beef knuckle for other uses if desired. Bring a large pot of lightly salted water to a boil. Soak the rice noodles in water for about 20 minutes, then cook in boiling water until soft, but not mushy, about 5 minutes. Slice the frozen beef paper thin. The meat must be thin enough to cook instantly.

Place some noodles into each bowl, and top with a few raw beef slices. Ladle boiling broth over the beef and noodles in the bowl. Serve with hoisin sauce and sriracha sauce on the side. Set onion, cilantro, bean sprouts, basil, green onions and lime out at the table for individuals to add toppings as desired.

SALaDS

MANDARIN ORANGE-PECAN SALAD

This quick and easy salad has become one of my favorites to serve to guests over the years. It's colorful, it's delicious. And while the recipe is based on using canned Mandarin oranges, it works well, too, with fresh winter citrus from the Rio Grande Valley when that wonderful stuff starts coming in.

2 cups mixed greens/spring mix
1 cup grape tomatoes
1 large cucumber, cubed
1 small red onion, finely chopped
¾ cup pecan halves or pieces

1 small can mandarin orange wedges, juice reserved
½ cup good-quality prepared poppyseed dressing

Ingredients

Serves 6

In a large bowl, toss the greens with the tomatoes, cucumber, red onion and pecan pieces. Add the mandarin orange wedges. In a separate bowl, whisk the poppyseed dressing with about half that amount of juice from the oranges. Toss the salad with the new dressing and serve.

WARM SPINACH-BACON SALAD

Years and years ago, some French chef taught me the trick of using the cooked egg yolks to emulsify the Dijon vinaigrette. It's the kind of trick French chefs tend to know. Everything else about this wonderful salad is pretty much timeless.

Ingredients

Serves
6

3 large eggs

8 pieces thick-cut bacon

4 tablespoons red wine vinegar

2 tablespoons olive oil

2 teaspoons sugar

2 teaspoons Dijon mustard

Salt and pepper

8-10 ounces young spinach leaves

1 cup prepared croutons

4 large white mushrooms, sliced

2 tablespoons minced red onions

Set eggs in cold water in a pan, turn on heat and bring to a rolling boil. After 2 minutes, turn off water and leave eggs in for 15 more minutes to finish cooking. Let cool enough to handle safely. Slice eggs in half to separate yolks from whites. Chop the whites. Fry the bacon until crispy, then drain on paper towels. Reserve about 2 tablespoons of bacon grease in the pan, along with crumbled brown bits on bottom.

Heat the reserved bacon fat and add vinegar, olive oil, sugar and mustard. While heating, add the cooked egg yolks and mash with a fork until incorporated into the hot dressing. Season to taste. Quickly combine the spinach, croutons, mushrooms, onion and chopped egg whites in a salad bowl. Pour the hot dressing over the top and toss until spinach is wilted. Divide over salad plates and serve immediately.

JUSTIN AT THE DOUBLE-WIDE

"How y'all are?" Justin Wilson asks, rolling out of his pickup onto the gravel and rising to full height beside his outboard-motored "Damboat"—so named for reasons obvious to anyone who's ever owned one. I was spending the day interviewing the Cajun humorist and cooking show host in a strange but wondrous way: bringing my wife and young children to his double-wide trailer on the Tickfaw River. For years afterward, in fact, every time my eldest daughter spotted his face and heard his voice on PBS, she announced they belonged to "my friend Justin Wilson." That alone was worth the drive.

A draft beer drawn from the porch keg and downed beneath a ceiling fan leads to a dip in the bracing river. Wilson, by no means a young man and enjoying what sounded like either a second or third career, climbed carefully down a ladder from his dock, skipping a swing on the rope nearby. The rope, he offered—speaking as a longtime safety engineer—was installed by an orthopedic surgeon to drum up business. After the swim we started cooking—for nearly twelve sweaty hours—outside which is how most of the best Cajun cuisine is prepared. I was writing it all in my notebook for *UPI*. It ended up being one of the most popular stories I ever wrote, running in newspapers across the United States, plus in Latin America, Europe and Asia. As Justin would have put it: "That's a lotta damn people, ah garontee!"

"The secret to Cajun cooking," he explained, starting an alligator étouffée before turning to an elk sauce piquante, "is that it takes a long time. You can put it on and drink a beer and have a good time. Cooking is fun unless you make it a drudge. My mother was a tremendous cook. You couldn't help learn from her because she had a tremendous sense of humor. If you ain't got a sense of humor, you ain't got nothing." He ponders whatever my question was a bit longer. "If you want to cook worth a damn, all it takes is common sense and imagination. But don't go imagining marjoram or coriander or however they say those things. Just imagine things like onions, bell peppers, parsley and Louisiana hot sauce."

Though Wilson's official address was in nearby French Settlement, he found himself spending more and more of his precious home time at the trailer. In fact, it had recently sprouted a veranda for sitting, a screened porch for cooking and a wooden shed for storing. The place struck me as a little piece of heaven, yet the heavy wooden wall that held solid ground together was a sobering reminder of time, the river and their constant erosion.

A TV producer arrived with his wife, along with (as though on command) an orthopedic surgeon with his wife. As stories and beer were passed around, the elk sizzled in a pan before tumbling into the sultry sauce piquante. It was dark beyond the cooking porch. Everything for tonight's dinner was bubbling in some pot or another, even as Justin supervised the stuffing of tomorrow's beef and pork roasts with garlic and green onions. The whole scene ended up looking like his production set—complete with a hungry, appreciative and (considering the beer) increasingly *live* audience.

"Hell's bells," Wilson said, wiping his hands on a towel that hung from his dungarees. "How you gonna reach back in the foremost portion of your brain unless you have an audience? I'm just a reflection of my audience."

PHANTOM RANCH SALAD

One of my life's favorite memories is riding some very sure-footed mules to the bottom of the Grand Canyon for an overnight stay at Phantom Ranch, going through climate zone after climate zone all the way down. For dinner at the ranch, we were served a salad with our pile of steaks, and I've never forgotten how good the dressing was. Happily, the wrangler who led our little group also scribbled down the dressing recipe. I still have that slip of paper.

Ingredients

Serves 6-8

⅛ cup cider vinegar
¼ cup sugar
½ teaspoon dry mustard
½ teaspoon salt
½ teaspoon paprika
½ teaspoon dried oregano
½ teaspoon Worcestershire sauce
½ cup vegetable oil

½ cup ketchup
¼ cup mayonnaise
1 tablespoon lemon juice
3 cups chopped iceberg lettuce or other
  salad greens
2 Roma tomatoes, chopped
1 cucumber, chopped

In a mixing bowl, whisk together the vinegar, sugar, mustard, salt, paprika, oregano and Worcestershire. Then add the oil, ketchup, mayonnaise and lemon juice, whisking until incorporated. Combine the lettuce, tomato and cucumber in a bowl and toss with the dressing.

SUMMER ORZO SALAD

Sure, everybody loves pasta salad, but it's usually a festival of mayonnaise. Not that there's anything wrong with that. But the people of Italy have a better pasta and a better dressing that'll taste great throughout the long, hot summer.

Ingredients

Serves
6-8

RED WINE VINAIGRETTE

¾ cup red wine vinegar

¼ cup fresh lemon juice

2 teaspoons honey

2 teaspoons salt

¾ teaspoon freshly ground black pepper

¾ cup extra-virgin olive oil

4 cups chicken broth

1 ½ cups orzo

1 (15-ounce) can garbanzo beans, drained and rinsed

1 ½ cups red and yellow teardrop tomatoes or grape tomatoes, halved

¾ cup finely chopped red onion

½ cup chopped fresh basil leaves

¼ cup chopped fresh mint leaves

Salt and freshly ground black pepper

Whisk together the vinaigrette ingredients until emulsified. Pour the broth into a heavy large saucepan. Cover the pan and bring the broth to a boil over high heat. Stir in the orzo. Cover partially and cook until the orzo is tender but still firm to the bite, stirring frequently, about 7 minutes. Drain the orzo through a strainer. Transfer the orzo to a large wide bowl and toss until the orzo cools slightly. Set aside to cool completely. Toss the orzo with the beans, tomatoes, onion, basil, mint and enough vinaigrette to coat. Season the salad, to taste, with salt and pepper, and serve at room temperature.

LOBSTER & AVOCADO SALAD

When you want something substantial for dinner at the height of Texas summer, and maybe something celebratory as well, it's hard to beat this chilled lobster salad. Even better, it replaces America's traditional reliance on mayonnaise with a flourish of great, cooling flavors from Thailand.

Ingredients

Serves 6

2 (2 pound) live Maine lobsters
2 tablespoons Thai fish sauce
1 teaspoon sugar
3 tablespoons freshly squeezed lime juice
3 tablespoons olive oil
1 small Thai chili, seeded and minced
12 large fresh Thai basil leaves, minced

2 sprigs cilantro leaves, minced
1 cup shredded Napa cabbage
1 bunch arugula, stems removed
1 small red bell pepper, seeded, and thinly sliced
1 large ripe avocado, peeled, pitted and sliced thin

Plunge the lobsters into a large pot of boiling salted water. Cover and boil for 10 minutes. Transfer the lobsters to a bowl and let cool to the touch. Using a clean kitchen towel, tear the claws and legs away from the body. Wrap the towel around the tail and twist, separating it from the body. Place the tail on its side and crush down with the palm of your hand until the shell cracks. Separate the meat from the shell and cut it into ½-inch slices. Using a lobster cracker, crack the claws and knuckles of the lobster and remove the flesh with an oyster fork. Use immediately, or cover and refrigerate for up to 24 hours.

In a small bowl, combine the fish sauce, sugar, lime juice and the chili. Stir in the basil and cilantro. In a large bowl, toss the cabbage, arugula, and bell pepper with ¼ cup of the dressing. Arrange the salad on 6 Asian style rectangular plates. Top with overlapping slices of the lobster and avocado. Spoon the remaining dressing over the avocado.

PRUDHOMME ON POINT

They are probably the two professional compliments that I treasure the most in my life—and both came from Cajun Chef Paul Prudhomme. One was that he always claimed to be the one who told me I should write about food. "You be good to food and food'll be good to you," he quoted himself. Though I didn't remember the encounter, I'm honored he thought I was worth claiming. The second was that he'd long considered the hour-long interview I did with him for my own *EasyFood* magazine in New Orleans the best article ever written about him. Sure, he must have known I'm a sucker for a pretty compliment, but that one has inspired me every day ever since.

I certainly wasn't afraid of talking with him, since Paul Prudhomme could and would talk with anybody. It's one of the things that made him a celebrity, in real life, in cookbooks and especially on his by-our-standards primitive Cajun cooking series. On another occasion, when I went to a taping at the PBS station in Baton Rouge, I was impressed that he kept a chair in which to take naps between recipe segments, while the set and cameras were being organized. To this day, I'm jealous of any nap taken by anybody anywhere.

But on *this* day, we talked about everything—include his "Fork in the Road" project that took him away from cooking Louisiana foods laden with butter and oil, about his years of anger at European chefs who prevented Americans from getting ahead, about how he learned that cooking for women equaled instant seduction (I was too married to do anything about it, but I took note. Hint: Apparently it only works if you cook like Paul Prudhomme) and even about early run-ins with the law I'd heard about from a friend from a small Cajun village near Paul's. But then, gulping a bit, I risked being Ted Baxter and essentially asked him "how it felt" to lose his wife Kay (the "K in K-Paul's) only months earlier at much too young an age, as though *any* age were not too young.

"I've always been a scattered person," he said, walking around the question until he found a doorway inside, "never satisfied and always reaching for something else, whether it was a new dish of food or a new business. Kay wasn't that way. Kay was in love with this restaurant. This was her restaurant in the sense that she would not allow it to change. She was in control, and I liked it that way. I would say jokingly, but I really meant it, that I cooked for her and created for her. As long as it satisfied her, we knew it was in the customer's direction. Now that's gone, and that's a huge void for me."

"It doesn't mean I want to give up the restaurant. It's a huge part of my life, and it was the beginning of everything that's happened to me in the last fifteen years. But I miss having that real solid connection, through her. Now if I want to have that connection, I have to spend every day, hours and hours here, to get the same I'd get from her in five minutes." When Paul slowed down I asked him about his smile, the one that brightens any retail space from the cover of any of his cookbooks. Was it difficult to make that smile happen, I asked, to get it right, after Kay's death? "It was relatively easy, because she would have wanted me to go on and do what I'm doing and have fun. That's a fact. I knew what she wanted to leave behind and I knew what she wanted me to do after she left. She would want me to do it the best that I could. When I had to be on, it was easy, because I could be on for her."

BLACK BEAN & RICE SALAD

If you're looking for a room-temperature salad that will accent any buffet table, you need to consider this satisfying Tex-Mex tantalizer built around the classic nutrition combination of beans and rice. If it seems at all like eating just to stay alive, you obviously haven't tasted it yet.

Ingredients

Serves 4-6

1 cup chunky tomato salsa
3 tablespoons olive oil
2 tablespoons freshly squeezed lime juice
¼ teaspoon ground cumin
1 tablespoon sugar
Freshly ground black pepper
1 cup cooked rice
1 cup cooked black beans, rinsed and drained

1 cup cooked corn kernels
1 cup garbanzos
¼ cup thinly sliced red bell pepper
1 cup chopped tomato
2 green onions, chopped
3 tablespoons chopped fresh cilantro
2 tablespoons chopped fresh parsley
⅓ cup toasted pecan halves
Lettuce leaves for garnish

Whisk together the salsa, olive oil, lime juice, cumin, sugar and black pepper. Stir in the rice, black beans, corn, garbanzos, bell pepper, tomato, green onions, cilantro and parsley. Stir in the toasted pecans. Serve at room temperature or chill 30 minutes before serving atop lettuce leaves.

SEAFOOD

AHI TUNA TACOS *with* AVOCADO SALSA

Inspired by Del Frisco's Grille, Tommy Bahama and the host of other successful restaurant companies dishing up their version of Asian-Latin ahi tuna tacos, I decided I needed to dish up mine.

Ingredients

Serves 4

DRESSING
3 tablespoons sour cream
2 tablespoons soy sauce
2 tablespoons sesame oil
2 teaspoons fresh lime juice
1 ½ teaspoons minced shallot
1 teaspoon minced fresh ginger
2 teaspoons chipotle paste

SALSA
2 ripe avocados, pitted and skinned, cut in ¼ inch cubes
1 roma tomato, cut in ¼ cubes
1 cup lightly packed cilantro leaves, finely chopped
¼ cup diced red onion
3 tablespoons freshly squeezed lemon juice
⅛ teaspoon salt
¼ teaspoon black pepper

TACOS
¾ pound raw sushi grade ahi tuna, cut into cubes
8 (3-½ inch) round wonton wrappers
Canola oil for frying
Cilantro leaves for garnish

Make the Dressing by whisking together all the ingredients in a bowl until fully emulsified. Prepare the Salsa by mashing together all the ingredients in a separate bowl. In another separate bowl, mix the cubes of tuna with some of the Dressing until lightly coated. Prepare the "taco shells" by heating the canola oil in a large pot to 335° F. With a stainless steel taco molder, submerge the wonton skins in the hot oil until crisp and golden brown, about 1 minute. Drain on paper towels. Let the shells cool briefly.

Assemble the tacos by filling the bottom of each shell with the Salsa, then topping that with coated tuna cubes. With a squeeze bottle, drizzle the remaining Dressing over the top and garnish with cilantro leaves.

SALSA SHRIMP & TEX-MEX CHEESE GRITS

By now, just about everybody knows that the Southern staple called shrimp and grits hails from the Carolinas. But it's safe to assume nobody up there ever thought of taking the classic on a Texas detour, adding a little tomato salsa to the wine-butter sauce and, even better, adding cheddar and Monterey Jack cheeses to the grits.

Ingredients

1 tablespoon extra-virgin olive oil
3 tablespoons unsalted butter
1 small onion, finely chopped
1 carrot, finely chopped
1 green bell pepper, finely chopped
1 (8-ounce) package fresh white mushrooms, chopped
1 tomato, chopped
2 green onions, chopped
1 teaspoon minced garlic
½ cup dry white wine
½ cup tomato salsa
Creole seasoning to taste
½ teaspoon black pepper
¼ teaspoon crushed red pepper
¼ teaspoon garlic powder
¼ teaspoon onion powder
1 pound medium-large wild-caught shrimp, peeled
Cooked grits, with blended cheddar-Monterey Jack cheese

Serves 4

Heat olive oil with 1 tablespoon butter in a sauté pan or wok. Sauté the onion, carrot and green pepper until they start to caramelize, then add the mushrooms, tomato, green onions and garlic, stirring until the mushrooms soften. Add the remaining butter, white wine and salsa. Add seasonings. Stir in the shrimp to combine with the bubbling pan liquid, cooking just until shrimp are bright pink. Serve with sauce atop the hot cheese grits.

NEW ORLEANS SHRIMP CREOLE

New Orleans was Spanish at one time, in between bouts of being French—and that means tomatoes were and always would be very popular. In general, anything called "Creole" shows this Spanish influence—not least since the word itself was born criollo.

Ingredients

Serves 4-6

½ cup finely diced onion
½ cup chopped green bell pepper
½ cup chopped celery
2 cloves garlic, minced
3 tablespoons butter or margarine
2 tablespoons cornstarch
1 (14.5 ounce) can stewed tomatoes

1 (8 ounce) can tomato sauce
1 tablespoon Worcestershire sauce
1 teaspoon chili powder
1 dash Tabasco or hot pepper sauce
1 pound medium shrimp, peeled and deveined
Steamed white rice

In a 2 quart saucepan, melt butter or margarine over medium heat. Add onion, green pepper, celery and garlic, cook until tender. Mix in cornstarch. Stir in stewed tomatoes, tomato sauce, Worcestershire sauce, chili powder and pepper sauce. Bring to a boil, stirring frequently. Stir in shrimp, and cook for 5 minutes. Serve over steamed white rice.

GRILLED SHRIMP TACOS

During my years of eating all over in Texas, I've certainly devoured my share of fish tacos. In most restaurants, I much prefer fish tacos to shrimp tacos. But if I make them with shrimp at home, the summery peach pico de gallo always carries the day.

Ingredients

Serves 4

PEACH SALSA
2 cups chopped peeled peaches
1 cup chopped tomato
1 cup diced red onion
¼ cup freshly squeezed lime juice, divided
3 tablespoons minced fresh cilantro
2 tablespoons minced green onions
1 teaspoon chopped seeded serrano pepper
3 tablespoons Muscat Canelli wine
1 teaspoon honey
¼ teaspoon salt

1 pound small to medium Gulf shrimp, peeled and deveined
¼ cup freshly squeezed lime juice
1 tablespoon minced fresh cilantro
1 teaspoon minced garlic
1 teaspoon chopped seeded serrano pepper
Salt and black pepper
8 corn or flour tortillas, warmed
2 cups shredded green cabbage
Additional minced cilantro for garnish

In a glass bowl or plastic bag, combine shrimp with lime juice, cilantro, garlic, serrano, salt and pepper. Marinate in the refrigerator for 2 hours. To prepare the peach salsa, combine all ingredients in a bowl. Toss gently so peaches and tomatoes are not damaged. Allow to sit for 10-15 minutes, so flavors can combine. Preheat grill and grill shrimp 3-4 minutes, turning once or twice. Serve shrimp wrapped in warm tortillas, garnished with peach salsa, shredded cabbage and a little more cilantro.

JAZZFEST CRAWFISH ROTINI

Whether it's for the original introduced at the New Orleans Jazz and Heritage Festival or just for any version using the bounty of crawfish season, Texans crave this pasta from the far side of the Sabine River. Here's my version that doesn't use any trademarked person's name, so you can enjoy it without inviting your lawyer. Unless you want to, of course.

Ingredients

Serves 6-8

1 pound of dry rotini pasta
1 onion, chopped
1 green pepper, chopped
1 stalk celery, chopped
1 carrot, chopped
5 cloves garlic, chopped
2 tablespoons olive oil
1 can Italian-style chopped tomatoes
Creole seasoning
Crushed red pepper

1 stick butter
1 pound of fresh, cooked or frozen
  Louisiana crawfish tails, undrained
Dry white wine
2 green onions, sliced
2 cups of half and half
Chopped parsley
Salt and freshly cracked black pepper
French bread

Cook pasta to al dente according to package directions. Rinse and drain well. Prepare a base by sautéing the onion, green pepper, celery, carrot and garlic in the olive oil until golden and caramelized. Add the chopped tomatoes, season to taste with Creole seasoning and crushed red pepper, and cook briefly. Purée this mixture in a blender or food processor. In a large pan, melt the butter and sauté the crawfish tails, incorporating any "fat" from the package for flavor. Deglaze the pan with white wine. When nearly all the wine has evaporated, stir in the green onions followed by the half and half, bringing to a boil. Add the purée. Quickly toss the cooked pasta in the sauce. Garnish with parsley. Season to taste with salt and pepper. Serve with crusty French bread.

JUDGING COOK-OFFS

Judging a cook-off can be great fun, whether it's the usual church or school fundraising affair or something closer to the national spotlight, perhaps with millions in prize money awaiting our decision. Judging allows us food journalists, whether we're broadcast or print, to stop flying our usual solo and rally our taste buds into that rarity of rarities, a group effort. There can be no doubt that the best part about communing with my peers always was—communing with my peers.

First-rate peers they were too—classy-cute Elizabeth Alston of *Redbook*, who later included several of my Mardi Gras brunch recipes in one of her cookbooks; irrepressible street kid Arthur Schwartz of the *New York Daily News*, talk radio and books; and the late cookbook legend Bert Greene, a Rabelaisian character with appetite and waistline to match. My new best friends spoke casually of "Julia" (Child), "Wolfgang" or even "Wolf" (Puck) and "Alice" (Waters), as though such folk might drop in for dinner at any moment—as indeed they might, if you lived at one of their houses. They often remembered their departed friend "Jim," removing any doubt that James Beard was the focal point of a movement that changed the way Americans ate and thought about what they were eating.

I essentially developed a policy of judging anything that didn't judge me first—meaning I decided it was important to my brand and perhaps to my soul to get "out there" as often as possible. This has made for many good and not-so-good eating experiences. One of the better ones, looking back, was being flown from New Orleans to Sulphur Springs, Texas, to taste 60 versions of vanilla ice cream at the National Ice Cream Freeze-Off. Still, the hat trick of all time landed on my doorstep one year, when I was invited to eat too much beef in Sun Valley, Idaho, too much chicken in Jackson, Mississippi, and, well, too much Pillsbury in San Diego, California.

I'd heard about the Pillsbury Bake-Off my entire life. Now, through some weirdness or other, I was helping decide who won it. They gave me one share of Pillsbury stock in a picture frame for judging, then bought the stock back from me a couple years later as part of some takeover. The framed certificate is still on my wall.

The most amazing thing about cook-offs was how your feelings (physical and emotional) evolved through the long day of tasting dish after dish after dish—there are no wine-inspired spit buckets at a food competition. That would be *too* gross. But, even though all the entries in these high-profile events had won regionally already, I would have probably used a bucket now and again. You got full, you felt fat, you became nauseous. And you wondered how any of this added up to a fair tasting whenever an excellent dish arrived—something you came to doubt would ever happen.

And then, invariably, one did. The table lit up, and we were like children on Christmas morning. Usually such excitement gathered around a single dish. Other times, there were several during the day, and we argued and horse-traded: "Would you go along with the Thai Chicken for Best Overall if I was willing to get behind Chicken Lasagna for Most Creative." A list of winners slowly emerged as did we feeling sick. At the National Beef Cook-Off in Sun Valley, I calculated that in about six hours I'd eaten three and a half pounds of beef.

Thanks to Pillsbury, it was in San Diego that Arthur Schwartz led a mini-mutiny, declaring he could never live with himself if he flew all the way from New York to sit in a hotel ballroom for a zillion-course, fancy-dress gala on closing night. He was *going* to find a hole in the wall for some cheap Mexican food if it took him all night, and if he had to do it alone. Arthur did challenge a small group of us to play hookie too. This was a moral dilemma as profound as any Huck Finn faced on that river. In fact, I thought of Huck. Since I knew what *he* would have done, I joined Arthur Schwartz and others in a couple of taxis.

We found a ramshackle quarter strung with bare light bulbs and cascading with bright food and mariachis. Uncounted cervezas and burritos later, we stumbled into that hotel ballroom just in time for dessert. There were approximately 800 people dressed up and seated quietly. And approximately 800 of them hated us. You see, just has Huck got a better ride on his raft than all those swells on the paddlewheelers, we'd just enjoyed the best meal at the Pillsbury Bake-Off.

GRAND ISLE SHRIMP BOIL

Today, especially when we "do Louisiana" in Texas, everything seems to be about the crawfish boil. But when I was growing up in New Orleans, the shrimp boil was king, except when people put on a crab boil. I never went to a single crawfish boil. Among other things, that was before the bizarre "Cajunization" of the New Orleans food culture in the 1980s, mostly by national food writers who didn't know a Cajun from a Creole. When I was a kid, you had to leave town to even find a Cajun—something we did each summer when we loaded up the car and headed south along winding Bayou Lafourche to a Gulf barrier island called Grand Isle. My father let his beard grow out, something insurance agents weren't allowed to do in those days. And on fishing trips that always started before dawn, my mother sat silently beneath her wide-brimmed straw hat in the back of the boat and caught more speckled trout than any of the rest of us. Afternoons were devoted to swimming, crabbing in the surf with chicken necks tied on string and dragging a long net called a seine through the shallows for shrimp. When we did the latter especially well, we did this for dinner.

Ingredients

Serves 6-8

Cold water
6 lemons
1 large onion, quartered
2 stalks celery, roughly chopped with leaves
1-2 bags of "crab boil" seasoning per pot
2 tablespoons Creole seasoning
2 tablespoons lemon pepper
1-2 teaspoons Tabasco or other hot pepper sauce

1 tablespoon apple cider vinegar
2 small red-skinned potatoes per person
½ pound smoked sausage per person
1 ear corn per person, cut into 2 inch pieces
½ pound medium-large raw Gulf shrimp per person

COCKTAIL SAUCE
½ cup ketchup
¼ cup prepared remoulade sauce
1-2 tablespoons prepared horseradish
2 tablespoons lemon juice
1 teaspoon Creole seasoning
1 teaspoon Tabasco or other hot pepper sauce
Saltine crackers

Fill a large pot ⅔ full with cold water. Squeeze the lemons into the water and toss in the rinds. Add the onion, celery, crab boil, Creole seasoning, lemon pepper and hot sauce; bring to a rolling boil. Add the vinegar to make the shrimp easier to peel. Reduce heat to medium, add potatoes and sausage and cook for about 20 minutes. Add the corn. When potatoes have softened to fork tender, add in shrimp and cook about 2 minutes, until shrimp are pink. Turn off heat and let the shrimp steep in the hot liquid 4 minutes more. Drain everything into a colander and run under cold water to prevent overcooking. Serve warm, or put shrimp in refrigerator for about 2 hours to chill. To prepare the Cocktail Sauce, stir all ingredients together in a bowl. Saltine crackers are mandatory.

DEEP SOUTH FRIED OYSTERS

When we finally get to a month with an R in it—which traditionally equates to a month with cooler temperatures—we can sidestep that old wives' tale and knock back some serious fried oysters.

Ingredients

24 to 36 Texas oysters, raw and shucked
2 eggs, beaten
2 cups cornmeal
1 teaspoon sugar

2 teaspoons salt
1 teaspoon pepper
2 tablespoons flour

Serves 4-6

Drain oysters. In a bowl, beat eggs; add drained oysters and let stand for 10 minutes. Mix cornmeal, sugar, salt, pepper and flour. Dip oysters in cornmeal mixture and fry in batches in deep hot oil or shortening—at about 370° F—until golden brown. Drain on paper towels.

BOIL FISH & JOHNNYCAKE

If you were a pilot for Chalk's International, the late and legendary seaplane airline, and waiting for your scheduled flight from Nassau to Miami or Fort Lauderdale, what would you have had for breakfast? If you were smart, you'd go Bahamian with this favorite island combo—as I watched two Chalk's pilots do with gusto many years ago.

Ingredients

Serves 4

JOHNNYCAKE
¼ cup butter
⅓ cup sugar
1 cup cornmeal
1 cup all-purpose flour
1 tablespoon baking powder
1 teaspoon salt
1 cup milk
2 eggs, beaten

BOIL FISH
2 pounds grouper or other white fish
2 cups water
6 potatoes, quartered
2 onions, quartered
¼ cup butter
1 lime, sliced
Salt and pepper to taste
Hot pepper to taste

To make the Johnnycake, preheat the oven to 350° F. Cream the butter with the sugar. In a separate bowl, sift together the cornmeal, flour, baking powder and salt, then add ¼ of that mixture to the creamed butter. Add the rest alternating with milk, stirring. When all is mixed, fold in the eggs. Pour or spoon in a buttered 9x9-inch baking pan and bake for 30 minutes. Let cool.

   Cut fish into 4 serving sized portions. Bring water to a boil in a saucepan and add all ingredients. Reduce heat and simmer for 20 minutes. Add more water if necessary. Increase heat to medium and cook until potatoes are tender, about 10 minutes. Spoon fish, potatoes and vegetables over a square of Johnnycake in a large bowl.

FLORIDA KEYS THAI SNAPPER

The juxtaposition of sweet-hot Thai chile sauce, cooling cilantro dressing and snapper from the reef off the Florida Keys—served up using yellowtail and mangrove snapper I reeled in aboard the Capt. Michael out of Islamorada—was nothing less than a taste epiphany. The fish was filleted by the captain on the dock and rustled up "Thai-style" by the kitchen of The Hungry Tarpon at Robbie's Marina. Here's the closest I can get at home in Texas to the magic of enjoying this dish beside the clear blue-green waters of the Keys that afternoon.

Ingredients

CREAMY CILANTRO DRESSING
½ cup cilantro, stems removed and roughly chopped
½ cup yogurt
Juice of 1 lime
1 garlic clove
¼ cup olive oil
1 ½ teaspoon white wine vinegar
⅛ teaspoon salt

CHILI SAUCE
¼ cup fish sauce
⅔ cup water
1 tablespoon sriracha chili garlic sauce
Juice of 2 limes
1 tablespoon sugar
1 teaspoon minced garlic
1 tablespoon cornstarch dissolved in 2 tablespoons water

FRIED FISH
8 fresh Gulf snapper fillets, 3-4 ounces each
2 tablespoons flour
1 teaspoon lemon pepper
½ teaspoon garlic powder
½ teaspoon onion powder
½ teaspoon paprika
½ teaspoon salt
1 cup panko Japanese bread crumbs
2 eggs, lightly beaten
Oil for deep frying
Black sesame seeds
White sesame seeds
Steamed jasmine rice

Serves 4

Prepare the Creamy Cilantro Dressing by puréeing all the ingredients in a blender or food processor. Make the Chile Sauce by combining the fish sauce, water, sriracha, lime juice, sugar and garlic in a saucepan. Bring to a boil, then remove from the heat. Preheat oil in a fryer to 350° F. Prepare three "stations" for each fish fillet: the flour mixed with seasonings, the beaten egg and the breadcrumbs.

In batches, dredge the fillets in the flour then shake off excess, dip into the egg and coat with the breadcrumbs.

Fry the fish in the oil just until golden brown, about 5 minutes. Drain on paper towels. Add the cornstarch mixture to the sauce and return to a boil. Transfer the hot fried fish to a platter and generously cover with the Thai chile sauce. Using a squirt bottle, decorate with the Creamy Cilantro Dressing. Sprinkle with black and white sesame seeds. Suggested portion is 2 fillets per person with jasmine rice.

GREEK FESTIVAL GULF SNAPPER

Whenever I make this super-simple recipe, I remember a long-ago fishing trip in the Gulf that produced an ice chest full of red snapper. You can make it in these amounts, or you can adjust it upward really easily when you've had a great day on the water. I make this every year when I can't wait for the start of Houston's Greek Festival in early October.

Ingredients

Serves 4-6

½ cup extra-virgin olive oil
2 pounds fresh snapper fillets
1 tablespoon Greek seasoning with oregano
1 tablespoon garlic powder
1 tablespoon onion powder
1 tablespoon lemon pepper

1 teaspoon crushed red pepper
6 lemons
3 ripe Roma tomatoes
Salt and pepper
½ cup dry white wine

Cover the bottom of a heavy baking or roasting pan with most of the olive oil, then lay the fish fillets in a single layer atop the oil. Drizzle with remaining olive oil. Sprinkle generously with Greek and all other seasonings. Thinly slice the lemons and squeeze over the fish, then arrange the slices across the top. Slice the tomatoes and arrange among the lemon slices. Sprinkle with more Greek seasoning, then salt and pepper. Pour white wine around the fish and bake in a preheated 400° F oven until fish is barely cooked through, 10-12 minutes. Using a spatula, carefully set fish atop pasta or lemony rice. Top with sauce from the pan.

MAINELY TEXAS LOBSTER ROLL

In the past few years, we in Texas have enjoyed a strange fascination with a food creation long associated with the state of Maine. Also known as Down East. And definitely known as Not Texas. There have been lobster roll restaurants and, in Austin naturally, a terrific lobster roll food truck called Garbo's that plies all those high-tech, well-paid business parks.

Ingredients

Serves 4

4 (1- to 1 ¼-pound) lobsters
¼ cup good-quality mayonnaise
3 tablespoons Fischer & Wieser Sweet and
   Savory Onion Glaze
Creole seasoning
¼ cup diced celery

2 tablespoons freshly squeezed lemon juice
⅛ teaspoon garlic powder
⅛ teaspoon crushed red pepper
4 top-split hot dog buns
2 tablespoons unsalted butter, melted
½ cup shredded Boston lettuce

To cook the lobsters, prepare a large ice-water bath. In a very large pot of boiling salted water, cook the lobsters until they turn bright red, about 10 minutes. Using tongs, plunge the hot lobsters into the ice-water bath for 2 minutes, then drain. Twist off the lobster tails and claws and remove the meat. Remove and discard the vein. Cut the lobster meat into ½ -inch pieces and pat dry, then transfer to a strainer set over a bowl and refrigerate until very cold, at least 1 hour.

In a large bowl, mix the lobster meat with the mayonnaise and Creole seasoning. Fold in the diced celery, lemon juice, garlic powder and red pepper until well blended. Heat a large skillet. Brush the sides of the hot dog buns with the melted butter and toast over moderate heat until golden brown on both sides. Transfer the hot dog buns to plates, fill them with the shredded lettuce and the lobster salad and serve immediately.

PALACIOS CATFISH CAKES

The development of farm-raised catfish in the Deep South over the past couple of decades has allowed this long-berated fish to become a delicate, flaky, clean-tasting experience that a lot of people love. This recipe, named for the area of Matagorda County that first tried farm-raising catfish in Texas, is one of my favorites.

Ingredients

Makes 8-10 cakes

1 pound fresh catfish fillets
Water
4 teaspoons oil, for sautéing
2 tablespoons onion, finely chopped
2 tablespoons green pepper, finely chopped
2 eggs, beaten
4 teaspoons Old Bay Seasoning
½ cup mayonnaise

2 teaspoon s Dijon mustard
1 cup dried bread crumbs
2 teaspoons freshly-squeezed lime juice
4 teaspoons Creole seasoning
2 teaspoons Tabasco or other hot pepper sauce
2 teaspoons dried basil, crumbled
Oil for frying
2 cups all-purpose flour

Poach catfish in a large pot of boiling water for about 15 or 20 minutes, or until the fish begins to flake with a fork. Drain poached fish in a colander, and place it on a baking sheet to cool. In a large skillet, sauté onions and peppers in oil for about 5 minutes, or until soft, and set aside. Take the cooled catfish and crumble it by hand in a large bowl. Add beaten eggs to the bowl of crumbled fish. Add cooked onions and peppers to the fish and eggs. Add remaining ingredients to fish and mix well by hand to create a cake-like mixture.

Form mixture into 6 to 10 equal-sized rounds and place on a baking sheet until ready to fry. In a cast-iron skillet or deep fryer, heat oil to about 350° F. Just before frying, thoroughly dust each catfish cake with flour. Fry the cakes in the hot oil until they are golden brown all over, rolling them frequently. Depending on your frying apparatus, this should take about 3 to 4 minutes. Drain the cooked catfish cakes on paper towels. Best when served immediately, but you can reserve them in baking dish in a warm oven until ready to serve. Serve with your favorite tartar sauce.

KEY LIME SEAFOOD PASTA

Here's one of the best things I tasted during my recent journey through the Florida Keys. The recipe is a favorite at Sundowners on Key Largo, where the Upper Keys start blending into the Everglades.

20 large shrimp, peeled and deveined with the tails removed
2 fresh Florida lobster tails, removed from their shells, and cut into large chunks
½ pound jumbo lump crab meat
2 tomatoes, diced
6 scallions, diced
6-8 fresh Key limes, juiced

4 tablespoons lightly salted butter
5 dashes Tabasco or other hot pepper sauce (add more or less to taste)
¼ cup white wine
4 cloves fresh garlic, chopped
1 pound penne pasta
Fresh grated parmesan cheese
Salt and pepper to taste

In a large pot, begin to boil water for pasta. In a large sauté pan, add butter, garlic, Key lime juice (to taste), white wine and Tabasco sauce, and stir over medium heat until butter has melted. Add pasta to boiling water and begin to cook until al dente (see instructions on package, should take approximately 12 minutes). Add lobster tail to butter mixture and sauté for 3-4 minutes until lobster chunks have begun to turn white. Add shrimp and tomatoes and sauté until shrimp and lobster are just done. Add salt and pepper to taste. Do not overcook. Add jumbo lump crab and scallions, stir gently so as to not break up the jumbo lump crab pieces, and remove from heat. Strain pasta. In a large bowl, place hot pasta and contents of sauté pan. Toss well and top with parmesan cheese.

CRAWFISH ÉTOUFFÉE

Like all my New Orleans favorites, I feel like this one got better when it hopped, skipped and jumped across the border to Texas. It retains all elements of the Cajun classic, but takes on a tad more bright flavors during its journey.

Ingredients

Serves 8-10

2 sticks butter
4 cups chopped onion
2 cups chopped celery
1 cup chopped green bell pepper
3 teaspoons minced garlic
½ teaspoon crushed red pepper
2 Roma tomatoes, chopped
¼ cup tomato salsa
¼ cup dry white wine
2 pounds peeled crawfish tails, preferably with fat
½ cup whole milk

2 bay leaves
2 tablespoons all-purpose flour
1 cup water
2 teaspoons Creole seasoning
1 teaspoon black pepper
1 teaspoon garlic powder
1 teaspoon onion powder
1 teaspoon Louisiana pepper sauce
4 tablespoons finely chopped parsley
¼ cup chopped green onions
Steamed white rice

Melt the butter in a large sauté pan over medium-high heat. Sauté the onion, celery and bell pepper until transparent, about 10 minutes. Then stir in the garlic, red pepper, tomato and salsa for about 3 minutes. Pour in the white wine and bubble until incorporated in the butter sauce. Add the crawfish tails, along with the milk and the bay leaves. Combine the flour and water until dissolved, then stir into the crawfish mixture. Add Creole seasoning, black pepper, garlic and onion powders, and pepper sauce. Bubble until thickened, about 4 minutes. Add the parsley and green onion and cook for 2 minutes longer. Serve over steamed white rice.

HALIBUT BRUSCHETTA STACKS

I've cooked this recipe for family and friends over the years using many of the most popular fish, including Gulf snapper and New England cod. But honestly, there's something about the flaky deliciousness of halibut with this lush blanket of bruschetta topping that takes the dish where I'm pretty sure I wanted it to go all along.

Ingredients

Serves 4

3 russet potatoes, peeled

1 tablespoon sea salt

2 tablespoons butter

¼ cup whole milk

Sea salt and freshly ground black pepper

1 teaspoon garlic powder

½ cup extra-virgin olive oil

1 small onion, finely chopped

1 (5-ounce) package baby kale, spinach and Swiss chard mix

4 Roma tomatoes, chopped

2 tablespoons chopped fresh basil

1 teaspoon crushed red pepper

4 (4-5-ounce) fresh halibut fillets

½ teaspoon lemon pepper

Roughly chop the peeled potatoes and cook until tender in boiling water seasoned with the 1 tablespoon of sea salt. Drain and transfer to a mixing bowl. Mash the potatoes with the butter and milk. Season with salt, pepper and garlic powder. In a sauté pan, lightly caramelize the onion in 2 tablespoons extra-virgin olive oil and then add the kale-spinach-chard mixture, stirring over medium-high heat until thoroughly wilted. Season with sea salt and pepper. Prepare the bruschetta topping by mixing the tomatoes, ¼ cup olive oil, basil and ½ the red pepper flakes in a bowl. Season with salt and pepper.

To prepare the halibut, season the fish with salt, pepper, lemon pepper and remaining red pepper flakes. Heat the remaining olive oil in a pan until hot. Add the halibut and cook until golden brown but not overdone, about 4 minutes on the first side, then carefully turn and cook 3 minutes on the other side. Make sure the mashed potatoes and sautéed greens are hot. Divide the potatoes into mounds at the center of dinner plates, then divide the greens over the mounds. Top each stack with a halibut fillet, pressing down lightly to stabilize the stack. Generously top the halibut with the bruschetta topping. Serve immediately.

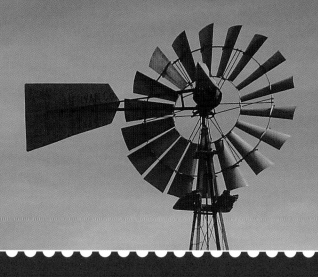

MEaTS

BORDER BLASTER CHICKEN & RICE

Named in honor of the Mexico-based, FCC-defying pirate stations of the '50s and '60s that turned Wolfman Jack and other DJs into borderland celebrities, this spicy baked chicken casserole is a Tex-Mex fiesta. Heavy on the Mex, I'm happy to report.

Ingredients — **Serves 8-10**

4 tablespoons extra-virgin olive oil
1 cup diced yellow onion
1 cup diced green bell pepper
3 garlic cloves, minced
5 chicken breast halves, cut into 1-inch cubes
Salt and black pepper
4 ½ cups chicken broth
2 (4 ounce) cans diced green chiles
1 ½ cups tomato salsa (medium or hot)

1 cup tomato-vegetable juice (such as V8)
3 teaspoons dried oregano
2 teaspoons ground cumin
2 tablespoons chili powder
2 cups long grain white rice
2 cups broken tortilla chips
2 cups Mexican blend shredded cheese
2 tablespoons chopped cilantro
2 cups sour cream for garnish

Preheat oven to 375° F. Heat 2 tablespoons of oil in a large pan and sauté onion with bell pepper until lightly caramelized, then briefly stir in the garlic and transfer into a bowl. In the same pan, with an additional 1 tablespoon of olive oil, brown the chicken on all sides, about 8 minutes. Season with salt and pepper. Add about ½ the sautéed vegetables, ½ cup of the broth, green chiles, 1 cup of the salsa, the tomato-vegetable juice and oregano. Bring to a boil, reduce heat and simmer uncovered for 20 minutes, until the sauce has thickened.

Meanwhile, heat remaining oil in a separate pot with a cover. Add remaining sautéed vegetables, along with cumin and chili powder. Sprinkle in the rice and stir to combine until rice begins to toast slightly. Pour in the remaining 4 cups of chicken broth plus ½ cup of salsa, and bring to a simmer. Cover pot and simmer until rice is fully cooked, about 20 minutes.

Transfer the chicken in its sauce to a large baking dish. Spread the cooked rice over top of chicken. Sprinkle tortilla chips on top of rice, followed by the cheese. Set the baking dish under the broiler and cook until all the cheese is melted and golden. Remove and garnish with fresh cilantro. Serve hot and bubbly with sour cream on the side.

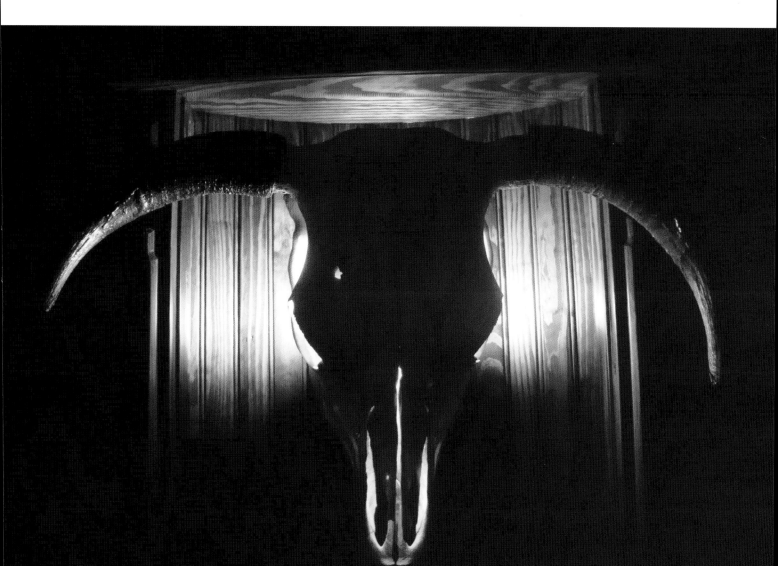

BUFFALO CHICKEN LETTUCE WRAPS

Everybody loves Buffalo chicken wings, that a great sports-bar feeder invented years ago at the Anchor Bar—in Buffalo, New York, where else? And just about everybody loves those sweet-hot soy-garlic-ginger chicken lettuce wraps served in Chinese restaurants. It required only some evil genius—no, not me this time—to combine the two crowd-pleasing, self-constructed foods for maximum flavor and fun.

Ingredients

Serves 6-8

1-2 tablespoons extra-virgin olive oil
2 stalks celery, finely chopped
2 pounds ground chicken breast
1 teaspoon lemon pepper
1 teaspoon garlic powder
1 teaspoon onion powder

½ teaspoon Creole seasoning
½ teaspoon celery salt
½ teaspoon crushed red pepper
About 1 cup Buffalo wing hot sauce
1 head iceberg lettuce, turn into full leaves
1 cup crumbled bleu cheese

Heat the olive oil in a large pan and stir in the celery, cooking about 2 minutes. Add the chicken, breaking it into small chunks with the spoon and stirring to cook through. Add a little more oil if necessary for browning. Season while cooking with Creole seasoning, lemon pepper, garlic and onion powders, celery salt and crushed red pepper. Pour on the wing sauce and stir to coat chicken evenly. Transfer to a bowl and serve with lettuce leaves and bleu cheese for wrapping at the table.

THE EMPRESS OF STEAK

You can do worse things in this life than learn how to eat steak from Ruth Fertel.

Unpretentious, gravel-voiced and heavily accented in a way any New Orleans native could recognize from the far side of the Superdome, the lady who'd turned a rundown steakhouse called Chris' into a high-end international corporation called Ruth's Chris was waiting. She was smoking cigarettes in a cluttered open area that apparently served as office to the tattered, now-departed restaurant on Broad Street, sitting at a table covered with clumps of separated cash, checks and credit receipts held together by rubber bands. She smiled, greeted me with that unforgettable voice (underlined by the visual of all her smoking) and waved me into a chair. I had to push aside a couple stacks of money to make room for my notebook.

The assignment came from *Hemispheres* magazine, then the wonderful in-flight published for United Airlines, and from its editor Randy Johnson. I loved *Hemispheres*, and it paid more than most in my life, so I was always pitching any story I knew half a thing about. Randy wouldn't hear of it. To give me an assignment, he had to believe it was "a true DeMers," a phrase no one else in my life has used before or since. This made it impossible to make much money, of course, or to travel the world on United, since Randy called only every year or two with something that had my name written all over it. Apparently, to Randy Johnson, Ruth had my name written all over her.

During the late-morning interview, we chatted about success in the restaurant business, since success is something people reading in-flights are thought to care about. With recent Ruth's Chris openings in Mexico and China (which, in those days, meant Cancun and Taiwan), the company's revenues had suddenly made Ruth the "most successful woman" in the industry. Randy wanted me to ask Ruth how and why.

"What I've learned," she said between drags, "is that I needed to hire people who knew a whole lot more about the business than I did. In the beginning, I did most things by myself, until I'd gotten up to about nine or ten restaurants." She thought a moment, about a story she'd surely told hundreds of times. "You see, I was a divorced mother with two boys, and I needed more money. I was working as a lab technician at a medical school that wasn't noted for its high salaries. I thought if I went into business for myself, I could make more money. One day there was this classified ad in the paper, and all it said was Steak House for Sale. I just went in and asked how much the owner, Chris, wanted. He said "$18,000." And I said "Okay." Using my home as collateral, I borrowed $22,000 from the bank."

Ruth and I talked about many things in our time together, including her efforts to learn about beef by visiting meatpacking operations in Chicago, her restaurant's rise to prominence feeding politicians, business people and sports figures who made her seem even more tiny than she was, and her own initial reluctance to grow beyond that single location. After a while, she asked if I wanted something to eat, and I don't typically say no. Looking at the menu, surrounded by a new version of the Old World dining room, with customers sipping chardonnay instead of their third martini, I told Ruth I'd probably be fine with filet mignon. She seemed, suddenly, quite disappointed in me.

"You *want* that?" Ruth said. It was such a weird moment, I had to ask what she meant. "Filet is okay, I guess," she said, "if you don't got any teeth. I go for the porterhouse, myself." She looked right through me, then grinned unexpectedly across the white tablecloth. "I like my steak with some *chew* on it."

When Ruth Fertel died many years after our first encounter, I realized that I'd been eating porterhouse steaks ever since. Whatever else we might say about this divorced mother of two growing boys, she *definitely* had some chew on her.

CHICKEN & WAFFLES

Since the combination now universally loved as "chicken and waffles" comes from the African-American soul food tradition, it makes sense that one of my favorite versions comes from the Breakfast Klub in Houston. Here's my home-friendly variation.

CHICKEN
Vegetable oil for pan-frying
¼ cup Tabasco or other hot pepper sauce
1 large egg, lightly beaten
18 chicken tenders
¾ cup all-purpose flour
1 teaspoon Creole seasoning blend
½ teaspoon garlic powder
½ teaspoon onion powder
Salt and freshly ground black pepper
2 green onions, sliced, for garnish
Warmed maple syrup

WAFFLES
1 ½ cups all-purpose flour
1 tablespoon sugar
1 ½ teaspoons baking powder
¾ teaspoons baking soda
¾ teaspoons salt
1 ¾ cups buttermilk
⅓ cup melted butter
2 large eggs
Green onions for garnish

To prepare the chicken tenders, heat the oil in a heavy-bottom skillet. In a bowl, whisk together the hot sauce and egg and toss the chicken to coat. In a separate bowl, combine the flour, Creole seasoning, garlic and onion powders and salt and pepper. Dredge the chicken tenders in the seasoned flour. Shake off excess and fry until golden in the oil, 2-3 minutes per side, turning once. Drain tenders on paper towels.

Make the waffles by stirring together the flour, sugar, baking powder, baking soda and salt in a large bowl. In a small bowl, whisk together the buttermilk, melted butter and eggs. Stir the buttermilk mixture into the flour mixture just until combined. Cook 6 waffles in a waffle iron coated with cooking spray. Serve each waffle on a plate topped with 3 chicken tenders. Garnish with green onions and warmed maple syrup.

RED BEANS & RICE

In the old days in my hometown of New Orleans, Monday was washing day—and that meant Monday became red beans day. Each Monday began with the ritual of putting a pot of beans on the stove. Different people had different recipes, of course. But those red beans slow-cooked for hours and hours, being declared ready just about the time everybody was starving for dinner.

Ingredients

Serves 10-12

1 pound dry red kidney beans
3 tablespoons olive oil
1 large onion, chopped
3 stalks celery, chopped
1 green bell pepper, chopped
3 cloves garlic, minced
2 carrots, chopped
Creole seasoning to taste
1 Roma tomato

1 pound smoked sausage, cut bite-sized
4 cups chicken broth
2 cups water
1 cup tomato salsa
½ cup tomato sauce
¼ cup white vinegar
1 teaspoon garlic powder
1 teaspoon chopped parsley

½ teaspoon oregano
½ teaspoon thyme leaves
½ teaspoon crushed red pepper
½ teaspoon ground cumin
Tabasco or other hot pepper sauce to taste
Steamed white rice
Chopped green onions

Soak the dry beans, either in cold water overnight or by combining with water in a pot, bringing to a boil for 2 minutes, removing from heat and soaking for 1 hour. In a sauté pan with about half the olive oil, sauté roughly half the onion, celery, bell pepper and garlic with all the carrot until caramelized, about 5 minutes, adding Creole seasoning to taste. In a food processor or blender, purée this mixture with the tomato until a thick paste.

In a large pot or Dutch oven, brown the sausage in the remaining olive oil, then add the remaining seasoning vegetables. Stir until lightly caramelized, seasoning as you go. Drain and add the soaked beans, chicken broth and water, followed by the salsa, tomato sauce and vinegar. Add all remaining ingredients and Creole seasoning to taste. Bring to a boil, reduce heat, cover and simmer until the beans are tender, 2-3 hours. Add more water if necessary to keep beans from drying out. At the end of cooking, for creamier red beans, ladle some beans onto a plate, crush with a fork and add them back to the pot, or purée some in a food processor or blender. Serve over white rice sprinkled with green onions.

COQ AU VIN

I often find myself pondering the culinary similarities between our own Deep South and the South of France, many of which can be captured in a single word—"more." I suspect it's the centuries of austerity living on unforgiving land that made us always tip a lot into the pot when a little might do. Either way, the line between classic coq au vin and downhome chicken fricassee will blur when you prepare this delight, developed when my friend, fellow writer and avid Francophile Holly Beretto, asked me to make her "something French" for her birthday.

Ingredients

Serves 8

1 (3-4-pound) chicken, cut in 8 pieces, skin on
Creole seasoning
2 tablespoons extra-virgin olive oil
4 slices thick-cut bacon, cubed
1 ½ pound carrots, cut in 1-inch lengths
1 large yellow onion, chopped
4 stalks celery, chopped
2 teaspoons minced garlic
¼ cup brandy
½ bottle dry red wine
2 cups chicken broth

1 tablespoon dried thyme
1 tablespoon dried parsley
1 teaspoon dried rosemary
1 teaspoon dried oregano
1 teaspoon dried basil
2 tablespoons butter
2 tablespoons all-purpose flour
½ pound frozen small pearl onions
1 pound mushrooms, quartered
Cooked egg noodles
French bread—optional

Preheat oven to 300° F. Generously sprinkle chicken pieces with Creole seasoning. Heat the olive oil in a large pan with a tight-fitting lid, such as a Dutch oven, and brown the bacon until crisp. Remove the bacon using a slotted spoon and drain on paper towels. Add the chicken, brown about 5 minutes in 2 batches, making sure you have turned it for even browning. Remove the chicken from the pan.

Add the carrots, onion and celery. Season with some of the remaining blend and cook until lightly caramelized, about 12 minutes. Stir in the garlic and cook 1 minute more. Add the brandy, red wine and

chicken broth, followed by all the dried herbs. Bring to a boil. Add the bacon and the chicken pieces, leaving chicken on top of the vegetables. Cover the pot with the lid and set in oven until the chicken is cooked through, 30-40 minutes.

Transfer back to the stove top over medium-low heat. Mash 1 tablespoon of butter with the flour and add this to the pan juices to thicken. Sauté the mushrooms and pearl onions in the remaining butter until browned, 8-10 minutes. Add them to the stew. Bring the entire mixture to a simmer and let cook another 10 minutes, so all flavors can meld. Season to taste with remaining blend. Serve hot over egg noodles and/or with hot, crusty French bread.

PEPPER JELLY GAME HENS

We forget sometimes that, since jellies are made by making a solid from a liquid over heat, heat can make them liquid all over again. And that's the simple science behind turning your favorite Texas jalapeño jelly into the perfect glaze for game hens, hams and a whole lot of other things.

Ingredients

Serves 6

1 tablespoon salt
2 tablespoons lemon pepper
1 tablespoon dried basil
½ tablespoon dried oregano
1 teaspoon garlic powder
1 teaspoon onion powder
2-3 tablespoons olive oil
6 (1 ½-pound) Cornish game hens, rinsed

2 stalks celery, each cut into 3 pieces
1 onion, sliced
1 orange, cut into 6 wedges
6 jalapeno peppers
1 cup jalapeno jelly
2 tablespoons butter
2 tablespoons brandy

Preheat oven to 375° F. In a bowl, stir together salt, lemon pepper, dried basil, garlic powder and onion powder. Rub olive oil on all surfaces of hens, then season with the blend. Fill the cavity of each with a piece of celery, slice of onion, an orange wedge and a jalapeno. Place on baking sheet with plenty of room in between. Roast in the preheated oven until the thickest part of the thigh registers 165° F on a meat thermometer, about 1 hour.

While the hens are cooking, transfer the jelly to a saucepan with the butter and brandy. Heat slowly until jelly has liquified. Brush hens with warm glaze during the final 15 minutes of cooking. Remove the roasting pan from the oven and loosely tent with aluminum foil. Let rest 10 minutes before serving.

BUTTERMILK FRIED CHICKEN

All of us in the South grew up eating fried chicken, sometimes made by our mothers and grandmothers, and sometimes made by various restaurants from fast food to casual dining. The result: there's very little agreement among us about what fried chicken is supposed to be. Here's my favorite Texas home version. I'll put in a drive-thru if you insist.

Ingredients

(3-pound) chicken, cut into 8 pieces
3 cups buttermilk
1 cup honey
2 teaspoons chopped chipotle chiles in adobo
8 cups vegetable oil

4 cups all-purpose flour
2 teaspoons cornstarch
Kosher salt and freshly ground pepper
2 teaspoons garlic powder
1 teaspoon onion powder
1 teaspoon smoked paprika

Yield 8 pcs.

In a large bowl, combine the chicken and buttermilk; refrigerate at least 24 hours and up to 2 days. In a food processor, combine the honey and chiles; blend until smooth. In a large Dutch oven, heat the oil to 275° F. In a large bowl, whisk together the flour, cornstarch, 2 teaspoons salt, 1 ½ teaspoons pepper, garlic powder, onion powder and paprika.

Working in batches, remove the chicken from the marinade and dredge in the seasoned flour; repeat. Add the chicken to the hot oil and fry until cooked through, about 12 to 15 minutes per batch. Repeat with the remaining chicken. Serve drizzled with the chipotle honey.

CZECH BEEF GOULASH

Prague is without a doubt one of the most beautiful cities on earth, long part of the gilded and glorious Austro-Hungarian Empire. As such, it is home to as much Art Nouveau as Vienna and, possibly, as much beef goulash as Hungary. Here's my version of a staple that was, literally and figuratively, all over the map during my recent visit to the Czech Republic.

Ingredients

Serves 6

GOULASH
1 large onion, finely chopped
2 garlic cloves, minced
¼ cup extra-virgin olive oil
2 pounds beef, cubed
1 teaspoon paprika
¼ teaspoon hot paprika (optional)
1 teaspoon ground marjoram
1 teaspoon garlic powder
1 teaspoon onion powder
½ teaspoon lemon pepper
Salt and pepper to taste
2 cups low-sodium beef broth

2 tablespoons tomato paste
½ cup water
1 potato, finely grated
1 pound smoked sausage, grilled,

DUMPLINGS
1 egg, beaten
½ cup milk
1 cup flour
⅛ teaspoon baking powder
1 teaspoon salt
4 -5 slices white bread, use stale bread,
    cut into small cubes (trim hard crust off)

Prepare the Goulash: Sauté onion and garlic in oil until translucent. Add meat with spices and sauté until brown. Season with salt and pepper. Add broth, tomato paste and water; simmer covered until meat is tender, about 1 hour. Add finely grated potato into the stew and simmer 5 minutes to thicken, stirring often. Serve with dumplings and pieces of grilled sausage.

To prepare the dumplings, mix together beaten egg, milk, flour, baking powder and salt until smooth. Add bread cubes to batter and mix well. Make two small loaves. Drop into large pot of vigorously boiling water. Cook 10 minutes, then roll dumpling over and cook an additional 10 minutes. Remove immediately from water and cut ends off to release steam. Cut into ½ inch slices and serve.

SHINER BOCK BARBECUED CABRITO

Down in South Texas, and indeed out in West Texas too, the state's love affair with beef eases up just enough to let glorious variations like cabrito find a spot on our table. To the surprise of many, goat meat is both tender and mild. It gets even more so cooked "low and slow," then slathered with my special Shiner Bock barbecue sauce. The photo shows a delicious cabrito variation cooked over mesquite at Sylvia's in Houston.

Ingredients

Serves 6-8

- 1 (5-6 pound) goat hind quarter, cleaned
- ½ cup prepared mustard
- 2 jalapeños, seeded and chopped
- ½ cup chopped cilantro
- ½ cup lemon pepper seasoning
- ½ cup chili powder
- 2 tablespoons garlic powder
- 1 teaspoon ground red pepper
- 1 cup butter
- 1 onion, peeled and sliced
- 1 tablespoon minced garlic
- 2 lemons, quartered
- 2 limes, quartered
- 1 bottle Shiner Bock beer
- 2 cups vegetable oil
- ½ cup Worcestershire sauce

Rub the goat completely with the mustard. Combine the jalapeños and cilantro with seasonings in a large sealable plastic bag and place meat in the bag, turning to cover with seasonings. Close the bag and refrigerate overnight. When ready to cook, melt the butter in a saucepan and cook the onions and garlic in a large saucepan until caramelized. Add the lemons, limes and beer. When the foam subsides, stir in the oil and Worcestershire sauce. Simmer for about 25 minutes.

Prepare the grill for indirect cooking, with soaked mesquite chips for smoke. Remove the meat from the marinade and place directly on the grill and smoke for 2-3 hours, basting regularly with the sauce. When the goat's internal temperature reaches 155° F, wrap it in foil and return to the grill until the internal temperature reaches 185° F. Remove from the grill and let meat rest for 20 minutes before carving. Serve pieces on a platter with barbecue sauce on the side.

GREEN CHILE PORK STEW

As I learned during a visit to record radio shows in Santa Fe, Taos and Albuquerque, green chile stew is the "national dish" of New Mexico. The key, of course, is the "chile" (as opposed to the "chili" here in Texas, a different thing altogether), using the fresh peppers in their green stage rather than their red. Chicken works every bit as well in this recipe; but in tribute to the colonizing Spaniards whose influence is alive and well here, I prefer the pork they taught the New World to love.

Ingredients

3 tablespoons olive oil
1 ½ pounds pork loin, cut in bite-sized pieces
2 medium onions, chopped
8 garlic cloves, minced
8 cups chicken broth
8 medium potatoes, cubed

1 cup crushed green chile
½ cup chopped cilantro
Salt to taste
½ teaspoon ground cumin
½ teaspoon oregano leaves
½ teaspoon freshly black pepper

Serves 10

Heat the olive oil in a large pot and brown the pork with the onion and garlic. Add all remaining ingredients, bring to a boil. Reduce heat and simmer until meat and potatoes are tender, about 30 minutes.

TUSCAN PORK & MUSHROOM STEW

As I discovered researching the TV cooking series with Damian Mandola and Johnny Carrabba, Tuscany raises some of the finest pigs in the world. This recipe, which pretty much proves it, has become one of the most-requested dinners at my house.

Ingredients

Serves 6-8

1 pound Italian pork sausage, hot or mild
2 tablespoons extra-virgin olive oil
1 ½ pound pork tenderloin, trimmed of fat
  and cut into bite-sized pieces
Salt
Freshly ground black pepper
Crushed red pepper to taste

2 tablespoons minced garlic
1 cup chopped carrots
1 cup chopped celery
1 cup chopped yellow onion
2 cups sliced mushrooms
1 cup chopped tomato
¾ cup dry red wine

Brown the sausage in the olive oil until almost cooked through, then add the pork cubes. Cook stirring occasionally until dark brown, 5-7 minutes, over high heat. Season with salt, pepper and crushed red pepper flakes. When meat is starting to stick to pan, stir in the garlic, carrot, celery and onion. Season again with salt, pepper and crushed pepper, cooking until vegetables turn golden and caramelized, about 10 minutes. Add the mushrooms and cook until they start to wilt, about 5 minutes, then incorporate the tomato and red wine. Cover and cook until the meat is tender, the flavors are combined and the liquid thickens almost into gravy. Serve spooned over polenta, or with penne or other pasta.

MIMI'S CHICKEN

I don't know about you, especially if you don't hail from the Deep South, but I had an aunt who wasn't really an aunt. She was actually my father's fraternity housemother in college. By the time I came along, she had reached "member- of-the-family" status enough to keep me with her at the frat house for days at a time all through childhood. I especially loved homecoming, when the cute coeds wearing corsages called me the "little freshman." Once I'd grown up a bit, I also especially loved Mimi's spin on traditional Southern Country Captain, made from boiled or roasted chicken, mayo turned yellow by curry powder and all.

Ingredients

1 roasted chicken (available at Spec's)
½ cup chicken broth
1 can cream of mushroom soup
½ cup fresh sliced mushrooms
1 teaspoon curry powder

½ cup mayonnaise
Grated cheddar cheese
Unseasoned bread crumbs
2 tablespoons butter, melted
Steamed white rice

Serves 6-8

Cut all the meat off the roast chicken, discarding skin and bones. Cut the meat into bite-sized pieces and combine in a casserole with the broth, soup, mushrooms, curry powder and mayonnaise. Cover with the cheese and breadcrumbs, brushing lightly with the butter. Bake at 350° F until golden brown, about 20 minutes. Serve over steamed rice.

BRAZILIAN PORK & BLACK BEAN FEIJOADA

It's been many years now since I first tasted the "national dish of Brazil" during a too-quick visit to Rio de Janeiro, overdosing not only on new flavors but on a new language, the Brazilian spin on Portuguese, which always works like Spanish except when it doesn't. I remember person after person telling me how Mamas used to make this time-consuming wonder for their families—but now, they all offered sadly, Mamas don't have time and families eat feijoada in hotels on Sundays. Except when they don't.

Ingredients

Serves 10-12

6 tablespoons extra-virgin olive oil

2 pounds pork shoulder, cut into 2-inch chunks

1 pound dried black beans, rinsed

1 pound smoked sausage, such as kielbasa, cut into 1-inch pieces

One 8-ounce smoked ham hock

1 large onion, chopped

2 dried bay leaves

2 cloves garlic

2 cups long-grain white rice

Salt and pepper

1 cup chopped flat-leaf parsley

Pickled jalapeño slices for serving

Heat 2 tablespoons olive oil in a Dutch oven over medium-high heat. Add the pork and cook, turning, until browned, about 8 minutes. Add 8 cups water, the beans, sausage, ham hock, ½ cup onion, the bay leaves and garlic and bring to a boil. Lower the heat and simmer until the beans are tender, about 2 hours; add water as needed to keep the beans and meat submerged. During the last 30 minutes of cooking, in a large pot, bring 4 cups water and the rice to a boil. Lower the heat, cover and simmer, undisturbed, until the water is absorbed, about 20 minutes.

During the last 20 minutes of cooking, in a large skillet, heat the remaining ¼ cup olive oil over medium heat. Add the remaining onion and cook, stirring, until browned, about 15 minutes. Transfer 1 ½ cups of the cooked beans to the onions and mash; stir into the stew and cook for 30 minutes longer. Discard the bay leaves and garlic cloves, season with salt and pepper and sprinkle with parsley. Serve over the rice and top with the pickled jalapeños and orange slices.

HERB GARDEN CHICKEN PARM

Sometime recently, for some reason, I decided that, for me in the big city, in the Green Acres phrase: "Farm livin' is the life for me." That meant a container herb garden on my third-floor balcony. Overalls definitely not required. I planted basil (of course, since even I can't kill basil—so far!), oregano, thyme, parsley and rosemary. Four of those five ended up in this recipe for one of my favorite Little Italy dishes of all time. You can probably throw in a little fresh rosemary too, if you want. But this is what makes sense for me.

Ingredients

Serves 4

⅓ cup extra-virgin olive oil
1 onion, finely chopped
1 stalk celery, finely chopped
1 carrot, finely chopped
Sea salt
Freshly ground black pepper
1 teaspoon lemon pepper
½ teaspoon crushed red pepper
2 (28-ounce) cans Italian whole tomatoes, preferably San Marzano
2 tablespoons minced garlic
2 tablespoons chopped fresh basil leaves
1 tablespoon chopped fresh oregano leaves

1 tablespoon chopped fresh parsley leaves
½ tablespoon chopped fresh thyme leaves
1 dried bay leaf
½ cup red wine
4 boneless skinless chicken breast halves
¾ cup all-purpose flour
3 eggs
1 ½ cups Italian breadcrumbs
1 ½ cups shredded mozzarella or mozzarella blend
Freshly grated Parmesan cheese
1 pound angel hair pasta, cooked al dente
Fresh basil leaves for garnish

Heat 2 tablespoons of the olive oil in a deep skillet or saucepan. Sauté the onion, celery and carrot until lightly caramelized, about 5 minutes. Season during this cooking with sea salt, black pepper, lemon pepper and crushed red pepper. Pureé the whole tomatoes in a blender or food processor, either until smooth or some chunks remain, as you prefer. Add the minced garlic into the caramelized vegetables and stir for 30-45 seconds. Pour the puréed tomatoes into the pan with the vegetables. Add the fresh basil, oregano, parsley

and thyme. Add the bay leaf and the red wine. Bring sauce to a boil, then reduce heat and simmer for about 45 minutes.

Preheat the oven to 400° F. Pound each chicken breast until it is uniform in thickness, about ¼ inch. Set up a three-step assembly-line (see note) by seasoning the flour with sea salt and pepper in a wide, shallow dish, lightly beating the eggs in a wide bowl and spreading breadcrumbs across a plate. Heat the remaining oil in a large skillet. Dredge each breast in flour, then shake off excess. Dip each into the beaten egg and then into the breadcrumbs, making sure to cover with crumbs and pressing lightly. Together or in batches, carefully place the chicken into the hot oil and cook, flipping two or three times until meat is cooked and coating is golden brown. Drain chicken breasts on paper towels.

Cover the bottom of a baking dish with the tomato sauce and set the chicken breasts on top of it. Cover the chicken breasts with sauce, reserving some sauce for the pasta. Generously cover with the shredded cheese and grated Parmesan. Place baking dish in the oven until the cheese is melted and bubbly, about 15 minutes. To make the top more golden brown, turn on the broiler for 2-3 minutes. To serve, toss the angel hair in the remaining warm sauce and divide onto dinner plates. Using a spatula or kitchen tongs, transfer the chicken breasts with sauce and cheese to each plate beside the pasta. Sprinkle with additional grated Parmesan and garnish, if desired, with additional fresh basil. Serve with pasta tossed with sauce.

NOTE: If you don't yet know the assembly-line trick of dipping almost anything in seasoned flour, beaten egg and Italian breadcrumbs, then you really should thank me. I learned it working on recipes with several Italian chefs on several of their cookbooks, and it's worth the price of a ticket all by itself.

BUTTERNUT SQUASH PENNE

This soul-satisfying pasta dish uses many of the best flavors of winter. It's inspired by a dish my youngest daughter Tessa remembers as one of her favorites from four years at Notre Dame, specifically from a restaurant called Greenfields where she worked.

Ingredients

Serves 4-6

1 butternut squash
2 tablespoons extra-virgin olive oil
1 tablespoon unsalted butter
2 stalks celery, chopped
2 carrots, chopped
1 large onion, chopped
2 cups chicken broth
1 cup milk

1 teaspoon garlic powder
1 teaspoon onion powder
Creole seasoning to taste
1 (14-ounce) can whole berry cranberry sauce
1 packed cup baby kale leaves
1 cup cubed cooked turkey breast
2 cups cooked penne pasta
½ cup pecan pieces

Preheat the oven to 375° F. Using a vegetable peeler, remove the hard outer skin of the butternut squash and cut enough of the orange flesh into bite-sized cubes to fill 1 cup. Slice or roughly chop the remaining squash and place in a roasting pan. Heat 1 tablespoon of the olive oil and the butter in a separate pan. Sauté the cubed squash until caramelized. Remove cubes from pan, set aside and sauté the celery, carrot and onion in the same pan until all are caramelized, then pour atop the larger pieces of squash. Place roasting pan in the oven until squash is cooked through and golden, about 40 minutes. Remove from oven and purée vegetable mixture until smooth, adding chicken broth and milk as needed. Season with garlic powder, onion powder and Creole seasoning, making butternut squash soup. You will have several servings of soup left over.

Heat canned cranberry sauce in a pot until it liquefies, then strain out the whole berries, collecting the red liquid in a bowl underneath. Heat the remaining olive oil in a pan and briefly sauté the kale until softened and dark green. Add the cubes of turkey and toss to heat through, followed by the cooked penne and caramelized squash cubes. Spoon in soup and fold gently until pasta is thoroughly coated. When heated through, add the reserved cranberries and pecans, tossing to incorporate. Serve hot on dinner plates. Drizzle with cranberry liquid and additional pecan pieces.

"**P**eople say, 'You're Bud Royer, you're the owner here,'" offers Bud, sitting on a stool by the register at Royer's Round Top Café, beside a plastic bucket of branded matchbooks topped with a paperback copy of Malcolm Gladwell's *Outliers*. "But I'm not. My *family* is the owner. They're the ones who've had to make this place go, and I stand on their shoulders." Bud smiles, even as the café's quiet starts tipping toward Saturday night cacophony. His eyes glisten. "My daughter always tells people, 'I went to Dad School.'"

To enjoy any level of success in Round Top, off anybody's beaten path between Houston and Austin, is odd enough. After all, the town's sign lists the current population as 90. Yet as though to make that 90 even harder to handle, there are more than 100,000 other folks who show up twice a year, in the fall and in the spring, for Round Top's big deal of an antique market. And there's an international music festival here too, plus a whole lot of affluent doctors, lawyers and stock brokers who show up for weekends to pretend they're ranchers. All this makes for a pretty strange crowd. But that's okay, since the Royer family has created a pretty strange café to take care of them.

The café is authentically quirky, the kind of place that every fake quirky restaurant on earth—read: Joe's Crab Shack and a thousand others—tries to emulate, never with total success. There's nary an inch of wall or ceiling that doesn't have some card, fabric, drawing or photo thumbtacked to it. Guest inscriptions and signatures complete the look, along with Royer's t-shirts ("Remember the Alamode," "Eat Mo' Pie" and, a Texas favorite, "No Pie Left Behind") hanging from the ceiling for buying. There's a soundtrack of '60s hits, loud enough to wrestle with any conversation and seem to be winning. At intervals, the crowd even hushes, for something truly iconic like "My Girl," as two dozen grownups visibly restrain themselves from singing along.

For all this studied chaos, the menu at Royer's Round Top Café makes the décor almost seem "normal." While it began life as a Texas café with Texas café food, today there's not a meatloaf or chicken fried steak in sight. The list is a series of high-octane self-expressions, neither upscale nor truly down, bursting with flavor and no small amount of butter and cream. A favorite sandwich, for instance, is the grilled shrimp

BLT, with a quarter-pound of grilled shrimp and another quarter-pound of thick-cut bacon, plus smoked mesquite mustard on a sourdough hoagie roll. And then there's the jalapeño poppers that are more like jalapeño *whoppers*, each pepper stuffed with Swiss, cheddar and cream cheeses, crabmeat and shrimp, then deep-fried and paired with lush cilantro ranch for dipping.

If such a fancy word can apply here, entrées run through several seafood and meat options that declare themselves "OMG"—from Tara's Grilled Gulf Snapper OMG to something billed as The Awesome Steak OMG—a 10-ounce center-cut beef filet on a bed of mashed potatoes, topped with portabella mushrooms and red onions with a creamy sauce of red wine and rosemary. And if *those* mashed potatoes aren't enough, you can always order some Bud's Smash, a mixture Bud concocted for himself one day ("Yes, I do like to play with my food") and customers kept wanting to "have what that guy's having." For the record, it's mashed potatoes with the café's creamed corn, red onions and crumbles of blue cheese. "People kept asking me what I called it," Bud remembers, "and all I could think of in the moment was Bud's *Slop*." He grins. "I finally decided that, in marketing terms, 'slop' wasn't exactly a great word for selling anything."

After 25 years of watching his kids grow up around the cafe, Bud can afford to be philosophical about the business and what exactly makes it tick. He knows what "slow" feels like in this restaurant, but he knows what "slammed" feels like a lot more often. Bud perches atop his stool this particular evening, scribbling people's names in a small tablet and assigning tables to parties of this or that size at this or that time. When he shares his "system" with an observer, he's told it's less like managing a restaurant than playing a really serious game of Tetris. He nods delighted agreement, then turns thoughtful.

"You know, the big thing here is the expectation," he offers. "When people walk in this door, they've just driven 80 miles to get a meal, and they've passed at least 80 other places to eat. And nearly all of them are repeat customers." Bud ponders this collection of evidence a moment, then hands down his verdict. "Food and service, they're the product, sure. But what we're really selling here is the experience."

COASTAL BEND PAELLA

This dish is half-great taste and half-nostalgia, since it references the Gulf Coast of Texas that curves south with ever more Tex-Mex flavor to the old shrimping port of Brownsville on the border. My plan here is to take Spain's classic rice dish on a similar journey, with a nod to the Cajuns and Creoles of southwest Louisiana while we're in the neighborhood.

Ingredients

Serves 12-14

2 tablespoons olive oil
2 chicken breast halves, cut bite-sized
1 pound smoked sausage
1 onion, chopped
1 red bell pepper, chopped
1 carrot chopped
1 tablespoon minced garlic
¼ teaspoon salt
½ teaspoon black pepper

¼ teaspoon crushed red pepper
¼ teaspoon garlic powder
¼ teaspoon onion powder
1 pound medium shrimp, peeled
1 tomato chopped
½ cup frozen green peas
¾ cup chunky salsa
2 (10-ounce) packages yellow rice mix
7 cups water

Heat the olive oil in a large sauté (or paella) pan and brown the sausage and chicken. Add the onion, red pepper and carrot, and cook until lightly caramelized. Add the minced garlic and stir quickly until golden. Season with salt, pepper, crushed red pepper, onion and garlic powders. Add the shrimp and stir just until pink, about 2 minutes. Add the tomato, green peas and salsa, stirring to incorporate. Pour in the rice and saffron seasoning, followed by the water. Bring to a boil, then lower heat to a simmer. Cover and cook until liquid is absorbed, about 20 minutes.

TEQUILA-MANGO BBQ RIBS

I love it when ribs go tropical. Here's one of my favorite renditions ever. And since you're pulling out the tequila to cook with, you might as well pour yourself a glass.

6 pounds pork spareribs
1 large fresh ripe mango
2 tablespoons chipotle chiles in adobo sauce
½ cup prepared barbecue sauce
¼ cup ketchup
¼ cup tequila

¼ cup freshly squeezed lime juice
2 tablespoons oyster sauce
1 tablespoon honey
6 cloves garlic, finely minced
¼ cup finely minced ginger
¼ cup chopped cilantro sprigs

Remove the membrane from the underside of the ribs. Then place the ribs in a rectangular dish or baking pan. To make the marinade, peel the mango and cut the flesh away from the seed. Combine the mango flesh and chipotle chiles in a food processor fitted with a metal blade and pureé. Transfer the mixture to a bowl, and combine with the barbecue sauce, ketchup, tequila, lime juice, oyster sauce, honey, garlic, ginger and cilantro. Makes 2 cups.

Coat the ribs evenly on both sides with half of the marinade. Marinate the ribs refrigerated for at least 15 minutes. For more flavor, marinate for up to 8 hours. Remove the remaining marinade to serve as a sauce for the ribs. To grill the ribs, if using a gas barbecue, preheat to medium (325° F). If using charcoal or wood, prepare a fire. Cook over indirect heat until tender, about 60 minutes. Occasionally during cooking, baste the ribs with extra marinade, stopping 15 minutes before removing the ribs. To serve, cut each side of ribs in half, into 3 sections, or into individual ribs. Transfer to a heated serving platter or 4 heated dinner plates, and serve at once accompanied by the reserved sauce.

MOROCCAN CHICKEN COUSCOUS

There was a time that a restaurant meal built around North African couscous was the first thing I wanted to eat in Paris—and the second, and possibly the third. Now that I've learned to make this simple, healthy chicken stew myself at home, I can settle for eating mostly French food in France. If you like extra heat, you have my permission to apply spoonfuls of harissa from that exotic part of the world.

Ingredients

Serves 6-8

3 carrots, cut in segments
1 pound Brussels sprouts, sliced in two
2 tablespoons extra-virgin olive oil
3 stalks celery, cut in pieces
1 large onion, roughly chopped
4 boneless chicken breast halves,
   cut in bite-sized pieces
Salt and pepper, or Creole seasoning

Mediterranean (or in a pinch, Italian)
   seasoning to taste
4 cups chicken broth
¾ cup chunky tomato salsa
1 can chick peas
Cooked quick or instant couscous,
   preferably plain

Cook the carrots and Brussels sprouts in boiling water (or in microwave) until just softening, then saute in olive oil with the celery and onion until vegetables begin to caramelize. Season with both blends. Remove from pan and cook the chicken pieces until golden brown, seasoning with both blends as you go. Return the vegetables to the pan. Add the broth, salsa and chick peas. Reduce hit to simmer and cook for 15-20 minutes, letting flavors blend and deepen. Serve over warmed cooked couscous on dinner plates.

TEXAS BEEF BOURGIGNONNE

Beef Bouguignonne is one of most people's favorite French dishes, a specialty of Burgundy where Pinot Noir is king. I have found that both of Burgundy's greatest hits taste really great in Texas.

Ingredients

Serves 8

1 tablespoon olive oil
8 ounces applewood smoked bacon, diced
2 ½ pounds chuck beef, cut into 1-inch cubes
Kosher salt
Freshly ground black pepper
1 pound baby carrots
2 yellow onions, chopped
1 green bell pepper, chopped
1 red bell pepper, chopped
2 teaspoons chopped garlic
½ cup Cognac
1 (750 ml.) bottle good dry red wine, such as Pinot Noir
1 can (2 cups) beef broth

3 tablespoons tomato salsa
½ teaspoon dried thyme leaves
½ teaspoon dried rosemary
1 teaspoon ground cumin
4 tablespoons unsalted butter at room temperature, divided
3 tablespoons all-purpose flour
1 pound frozen pearl onions
1 pound fresh mushrooms, roughly chopped
2 tomatoes, chopped
Country bread or Sour Dough, toasted or grilled and rubbed with garlic clove
½ cup chopped fresh parsley, optional

Preheat the oven to 250° F. Heat the olive oil in a large Dutch oven. Add the bacon and cook over medium heat for 10 minutes, stirring occasionally, until the bacon is lightly browned. Remove the bacon with a slotted spoon to a large plate. Dry the beef cubes with paper towels and then sprinkle them with salt and pepper. In single layer batches, sear the beef in the hot oil for 3 to 5 minutes, turning to brown on all sides. Remove the seared cubes to the plate with the bacon and continue searing until all the beef is browned.

Toss the carrots, onions, sweet peppers, 1 tablespoon of salt and 2 teaspoons of pepper into the pan, and cook for 10 to 15 minutes, stirring occasionally, until the onions are lightly browned. Add the garlic, and cook for 1 more minute. Add the Cognac. Put the meat and bacon back into the pot with the juices. Add the

bottle of wine plus enough beef broth to almost cover the meat. Add the salsa, thyme, rosemary and cumin. Bring to a simmer, cover the pot with a tight-fitting lid, and place it in the oven for about 1 ¼ hours or until the meat and vegetables are very tender when pierced with a fork.

Combine 2 tablespoons of butter and the flour with a fork and stir into the stew. In a separate pan, sauté the pearl onions, mushrooms and tomatoes in 2 tablespoons of butter for 10 minutes until lightly browned and then add to the stew. Bring the stew to a boil on top of the stove, then lower the heat and simmer for 15 minutes. Season to taste. To serve, toast the bread in the toaster or oven. Rub each slice on 1 side with a cut clove of garlic. For each serving, spoon the stew over a slice of bread and sprinkle with parsley.

PERI-PERI GRILLED CHICKEN BREAST

Everybody the world over loves spicy chicken, but a special plot twist has been applied by peri-peri, the Swahili word for the hot peppers brought to Angola and Mozambique a long time ago by Portuguese explorers and settlers. In Washington, D.C., and London, as well as a few other places around the globe, there are restaurants called Nando's that do something like this.

Ingredients

Serves 8

GLAZE
3 tablespoons butter
3 tablespoons finely chopped fresh cilantro
2 garlic cloves, minced
2 tablespoons peri-peri hot pepper sauce, such as Nando's
2 tablespoons fresh lemon juice

¼ cup chopped fresh cilantro
1 2-inch piece fresh ginger, peeled, thinly sliced
1 large shallot, peeled, quartered
3 garlic cloves, peeled
½ cup peri-peri hot pepper sauce
¼ cup extra-virgin olive oil, plus additional for brushing
¼ cup fresh lemon juice
1 teaspoon kosher salt
1 teaspoon freshly ground black pepper
8 boneless, skinless chicken breasts

To make the glaze, melt butter in small saucepan over medium-high heat. Add cilantro and garlic; cook until garlic begins to brown, about 2 minutes. Add peri-peri sauce and lemon juice. Reduce heat to medium-low; simmer 2 minutes.

Finely chop cilantro, ginger, shallot and garlic in food processor. Add peri-peri sauce, ¼ cup oil, lemon juice, coarse salt and pepper; process marinade to blend. Place chicken in a bowl or baking dish and pour marinade over the top. Cover and chill at least 4 hours or overnight, turning chicken occasionally. When ready to cook, preheat a grill and brush grate with oil. Remove chicken from marinade and arrange on the grill. Cover and cook, turning a few times, 10-12 minutes. Brush with the glaze near the end of cooking. Serve with French fries and a salad.

SUPER TRIO CASHEW CHICKEN

I've been making (or trying to make) my own Chinese food so many years that you'd thing I was born with a wok in my hand. I wasn't. It's been a long road. But when I experimented by adding a storebought mix of baby kale, spinach and chard (sold as Super Trio) to the wok with my cashew chicken, I decided the long road was worth it.

Ingredients — **Serves 4**

1 pound ground chicken
1 tablespoon extra-virgin olive oil
1 tablespoon minced garlic
1 teaspoon minced fresh ginger
1 teaspoon crushed red pepper
1 packed cup kale-spinach-chard mix
3 tablespoons soy sauce

1 tablespoon sugar
2 teaspoons dry sherry
1 teaspoon sesame oil
½ tablespoon cornstarch, dissolved in water
¾ cup cashew nuts
Steamed white rice

Heat a wok and stir the chicken until almost cooked through with the olive oil, garlic, ginger and red pepper. Add the kale mixture and stir just until wilted, about 2 minutes. In a bowl, combine the soy sauce, sugar, sherry and sesame oil and pour into the wok. Add the dissolved cornstarch and stir until mixture bubbles over the heat. Stir in the cashews. Serve hot over rice.

MARFA MEATLOAF

The key to this dish, created by my fictional alter ego Chef Brett Baldwin of Mesquite Restaurant in Marfa, is the use of pulverized tortilla chips where the breadcrumbs typically (but much more boringly) are. And if you're paying attention, you'll note that "taco seasoning" would work instead of the itemized spices. I often use taco seasoning in such cases because it tastes so good, but it's probably totally uncool to admit it.

Ingredients

Serves 6-8

2 pounds ground beef
2 cups pulverized (pulsed in a food processor) tortilla chips
1 onion, finely chopped
1 egg, lightly beaten
1 cup plus 1 cup chunky tomato salsa
1 teaspoon ground cumin

½ teaspoon garlic powder
½ teaspoon onion powder
½ teaspoon ground oregano
Salt and black pepper
1 cup beef stock
1 teaspoon instant roux (or cornstarch dissolved in 1 teaspoon part water)

In a mixing bowl, combine the beef with the tortilla chips, onion and egg. Stir to incorporate the 1 cup salsa along with the cumin, garlic and onion powders, and oregano. Season with salt and pepper. Transfer meat mixture to a loaf pan and cook in a preheated 380° F oven until crispy on top and done, about 1 hour. Meanwhile, heat the beef stock with the remaining salsa in a pan. When it bubbles, add the instant roux or cornstarch, letting the sauce thicken into a light gravy. Reduce heat to a simmer. When meatloaf is cooked, let cool until safe to handle and carefully slice it into servings. Transfer to the gravy. Let simmer for at least 30 minutes before serving.

SHINER BOCK SOB STEW

Well, that's not quite the real name this beef stew picked up in the Old West, but it's enough to give you the idea. On the trail, this stew was made with meat plus many organs—including something truly gross called the "marrow gut." Thankfully, this modernized version is a bit sanitized as well. And as any cowboy who actually says "son of a *gun*" would happily tell you: It's *dang* good!

Ingredients

Serves 8-10

3 pound boneless beef stew meat, fat trimmed

2 onions, chopped

2 garlic cloves, minced

1 tablespoon Worcestershire sauce

⅓ cup dry red wine

⅓ cup all-purpose flour

2 tablespoon sugar

1 teaspoon dried thyme

¼ teaspoon black pepper

¼ teaspoon ground red pepper

1 quart regular strength beef broth

12 ounces Shiner Bock beer (1 can or bottle)

2 russet potatoes, peeled, cut into
 1 ½ inch chunks

4 carrots, sliced ½ inch thick

2 cup coarsely chopped cabbage

1 cup coarsely chopped celery

2 bay leaves

Salt to taste

Tabasco or other hot pepper sauce to taste

In a 6-8 quart pan or Dutch oven, combine beef, onions, garlic and Worcestershire. Cover and cook over medium-high heat for 30 minutes. Uncover and stir often until liquid evaporates and its residue turns dark brown. Add wine and stir to release browned bits. Smoothly mix flour, sugar, thyme and peppers with one cup of the broth. Add to beef along with the remaining broth. Add beer, potatoes, carrots, cabbage, celery and bay leaves. Adjust heat to maintain a simmer. Cover and simmer until meat is very tender when pierced. Season with salt.

Tom Perini of Buffalo Gap travels with the ghost of Texas past—an elusive spirit born of cattle drives, dust-driven ranches and especially cowboys, back when that was a job rather than a fashion statement.

Perini, recognized master of chuck wagon cooking, parlayed the simplest ranch fare into a successful restaurant in a town of only 499 and a catering business that serves presidents, prime ministers and kings. He has demonstrated his brand of chuck wagon cooking across the United States, as in faraway settings like Japan and Poland. Most of all, though, Tom wants to preach the gospel of Texas past to the children of Texas future.

"It's a simple kind of Texas food," he drawled at me slowly for an article in the *Houston Chronicle* in 2002. "When you look at real Texas food, this was the base. When people say they're 'meat and potatoes,' that would reflect the chuck wagon."

In that first interview in Houston, and during many subsequent trips to Buffalo Gap just outside Abilene, I came to admire Tom and enjoy his company immensely. He always seemed slightly surprised by the attention and success he's enjoyed—that being the "Aw shucks" portion of both personality and persona. Yet he also emerged as an ambitious and shrewd businessman, a tireless worker and a bit of a visionary. He understood, and as of this writing still understands, that part of the Texas cowboy mythology that appeals to all men every much as it does to all women. In the hyphenated world of immigrant cultures in America, Tom taught me that we are all Part-Cowboy.

The years 1865 to 1880 are essential to Tom, who marvels at the romantic value Hollywood has attached to cattle drives when they really took place in only twenty-five years before the arrival of the railroads in Texas. During this period Charles Goodnight (Texas cattleman and trail driver of the famed Goodnight-Loving Trail— you have to love that name!) is credited with creating the chuck wagon. It happened in 1866, as Goodnight and partner Oliver Loving prepared to take a herd of 2,000 longhorns from near Fort Belknap in north Texas to Denver. Goodnight purchased a government wagon and had it rebuilt according to his design in the toughest wood available, known as bois d'arc. The first "chuck wagon"—yes, Chuck as in

Charles—was ready to roll.

The primary feature of the chuck wagon, Tom explained, was the chuck box—often made to the individual cook's specifications, with cupboards, drawers, shelves and enough hooks to hold just about everything the cook might need. A well-stocked chuck box would hold salt, pepper, flour, beans, sugar, molasses, coffee, lard, canned goods, salsa, dried fruit, bacon and perhaps a little fresh beef wrapped in a tarp. Yet the wagon was more than a pantry for non-perishable foods. It was storage for tableware, basic medical supplies and a coffee grinder nailed to some part of the side.

Cowboy grub could be flavorless, so chuck wagon cooks started experimenting with canned tomatoes and Mexican-style salsas. These products became a practical way to add flavor to everything, from eggs at sunrise to beans and brisket at dusk. Trail riders did have a sweet tooth, Tom assured me, especially when it came to their favorite sweet: A Navy recipe called Spotted Pup made with rice, raisins and cinnamon. One cook ran out of cinnamon on a long drive and discovered that substituting Copenhagen snuff worked just fine once dessert was served with as strong cup of Arbuckle's coffee.

Tom grew up raising cattle on the Perini Cattle Co. spread around Buffalo Gap, with a part of the old Goodnight-Loving Trail running through it. He discovered an affection for chuck wagon cooking early own, letting that evolve into a chuck wagon catering business in the early 1970s and into the Perini Ranch Steakhouse in 1983. I never fail to visit with Tom and his wife Lisa—not to mention eating a great meal in a wild and rustic setting—anytime life takes me to Buffalo Gap. It's a great steakhouse, a slice of history, a Texas treasure. And, as Tom told me in that first interview and most times ever since: "It's a real nice joint."

TEXAS FRITO PIE FRITTATA

Really now, who in Texas doesn't love Frito Pie? Next time, though, try your Frito Pie as a frittata. Talk about a Lone Star brunch!

Ingredients

Serves 10-12

2 pounds lean ground beef
2 tablespoons minced garlic
1 cup diced onion
½ cup finely chopped carrot
1 ½ cups chopped green chiles, such as Hatch (fresh or canned)
1 can cooked navy beans
1 cup chicken stock
1 cup plus ½ cup chunky tomato salsa

1 tablespoon chili powder
1 tablespoon ground cumin
1 tablespoon dried oregano
1 teaspoon garlic powder
1 teaspoon onion powder
2 teaspoons ground black pepper
½ teaspoon white pepper
Pinch red pepper flakes
½ bunch cilantro leaves, chopped
12 eggs

½ cup plus 1 cup grated cheddar cheese
½ cup plus 1 cup grated Monterey Jack cheese
1 cup chopped red bell pepper
½ cup chopped green onions
Fritos
1 raw onion, chopped

Brown the ground beef in a large pot, then drain off as much fat as you can. Add the garlic, onion and chiles and sauté with the beef for 5 minutes. Add the beans, chicken stock and salsa and bring to a boil over high heat. Season with the chili powder, cumin, oregano, garlic and onion powders, pepper, white pepper, red pepper flakes and cilantro. Lower the heat to medium and cook, stirring occasionally, for approximately 1 hour.

Meanwhile, preheat the oven to 375° F. Make the frittata by beating the eggs until frothy and folding in the ½ cup of each cheese, bell pepper, green onion and remaining ½ cup salsa. Pour mixture into a large, deep casserole or baking dish—the eggs should reach no more than ⅓ up the side. Bake until set, risen slightly and almost cooked through, about 20 minutes. Remove dish from the oven and top with Fritos, chopped onion and the chili. Cover with the remaining 1 cup of each cheese. Return to the oven until the cheese melts and turns golden brown, 15-20 minutes. Serve hot with additional Fritos for fancy garnish.

SOUVLAKI BEEF STEW

I usually make this Greek-flavored stew the day after Houston's Original Greek Festival that's held the first weekend in October, picking up a few extra skewers of marinated and grilled beef tenderloin souvlaki on my way out the gate. You can, however, recreate the wonderful Mediterranean flavors of Greek Fest wherever you happen to be, any day of the year.

MARINADE
½ cup red wine
2 teaspoons chopped oregano
1 teaspoon minced garlic
1 teaspoon kosher salt
½ teaspoon freshly ground black pepper
½ teaspoon crushed red pepper
Juice of ½ of a lemon
½ cup extra-virgin olive oil
2 bay leaves

2 pound beef tenderloin or sirloin, cut bite-sized
3 tablespoons extra-virgin olive oil
2 onions, chopped
1 cup chopped celery
6 carrots, roughly chopped
1-2 cups Brussels sprouts
1 teaspoon minced garlic
1 cup red wine
2 cups beef broth
1 cup chopped tomatoes
2 cups canned chick peas
2 teaspoons Creole seasoning
2 teaspoons chopped fresh thyme leaves
1 teaspoon onion powder
1 teaspoon garlic powder
1 teaspoon lemon pepper
1 teaspoon chopped parsley
1 teaspoon chopped oregano
½ teaspoon ground cumin
Couscous, egg noodles or polenta

Combine the marinade ingredients in a plastic freezer bag or bowl with a cover. Add the chunks of beef and marinate in the refrigerator for 24 hours. When ready to cook, remove the beef from the marinade and either grill on skewers for extra *souvlaki* flavor or brown in stock pot or Dutch oven. Remove from heat. Discard marinade. Add olive oil to pot and cook the onion, celery and carrot until they begin to caramelize, then add Brussels sprouts and cook until they caramelize too. Add the minced garlic and stir about a minute more, releasing the flavor. Add the beef and all remaining ingredients. Reduce heat and cook until all vegetables are tender, about 20 minutes. Serve over couscous, egg noodles or polenta.

THUNDER HEART BISON FAJITAS

I'll never forget the time I made the trek deep into South Texas to witness a bison harvest with longtime rancher Hugh Fitzsimons of Thunder Heart. The experience inspired an entire recurring theme in my West Texas crime novels featuring Chef Brett and his hulking Native American sidekick Jud Garcia—not to mention this terrific spin on Tex-Mex fajitas.

Ingredients

1 pound Texas bison skirt or flank steak
Juice of 3 limes
½ teaspoon salt
½ teaspoon garlic powder
½ teaspoon chili powder
½ teaspoon black pepper
1 large onion, sliced

1 large green bell pepper, sliced
1 large tomato, chopped
Prepared guacamole
Prepared sour cream
Prepared tomato salsa
4 corn or flour tortillas, warmed

Serves 6-8

Using a mallet, pound the meat to about ½ inch thick, then place in a plastic bag with the lime juice, salt, garlic powder, chili powder and black pepper. Seal bag and marinate in the refrigerator about 8 hours. When ready to grill, caramelized the onion and bell pepper slices in a pan with a little olive oil. Remove the meat from the marinade and grill over mesquite coals to about medium rare, 2-3 minutes per side. Thinly slice the meat. Serve the bison slices atop the caramelized onion and bell pepper, with chopped tomato, guacamole, sour cream, salsa and warm tortillas on the side.

SIDes

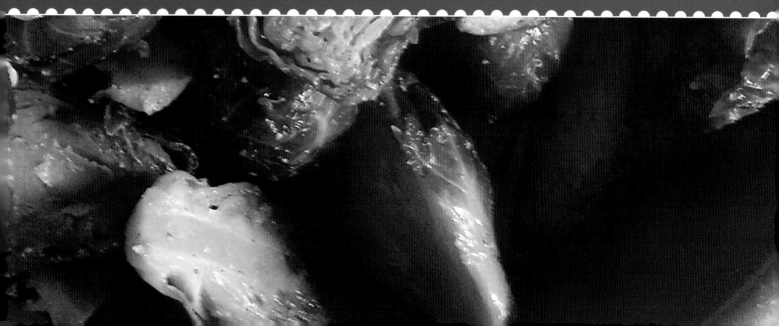

RODEO BAKED BEANS

You can't live in Texas very long—or pursue Texas barbecue with any seriousness—without falling more than a little bit in love with beans. We may not like them in our chili, but we love them practically everywhere else.

Ingredients

2 (15-ounce) cans pork and beans
⅔ cup brown sugar
½ cup chopped onion
½ cup prepared ketchup
1 tablespoon prepared yellow mustard

1 teaspoon Worcestershire sauce
1 teaspoon red wine vinegar
Salt and black pepper to taste
2 slices bacon, chopped

Serves 8

Combine the pork and beans with the brown sugar, onion, ketchup, mustard, Worcestershire and vinegar in a baking dish and season with salt and pepper. Mix in the chopped bacon and set dish in a preheated 350° F oven (You can also set the dish in the smoker, as many barbecue places do). Cook until the sauce is thickened, about 1 hour.

HOLIDAY STUFFING

I never much cared about traditional turkey stuffing (or, if baked separately from turkey, "dressing")—until my daughter showed me an old-fashioned recipe passed down within her new husband's family. I was intrigued, as usual, by such a generational food narrative and decided to figure out how to make it myself. Along the way, I let my beloved flavors of Louisiana and Texas sneak in. I never hate it when that happens.

Ingredients

Serves 14-16

Extra-virgin olive oil
1 onion, finely chopped
1 red bell pepper, finely chopped
2 carrots, finely chopped
2 stalks celery, finely chopped
4 fully cooked breakfast sausage patties, chopped
1 tablespoon minced garlic
2 day-old baguettes, cut or torn into cubes

6 slices whole-wheat bread, one or more types, cut into cubes
1-2 cups chicken broth
2 tablespoons rubbed sage
1 teaspoon garlic powder
1 teaspoon onion powder
1 teaspoon lemon pepper
Creole seasoning to taste

Preheat the oven to 350° F. Sauté the onion, bell pepper, carrot and celery in olive oil over medium-high heat until soft and caramelized, about 10 minutes. Add the cooked sausage and the garlic, stirring to blend with the vegetables. In a large bowl, combine this mixture with all the bread, adding broth and turning with a fork or spoon until completely moistened. Season with sage, garlic and onion powder, lemon pepper and Creole seasoning to taste—you can taste and adjust the mixture, as everything is fully cooked. Transfer to a large baking dish and gently press down to remove excess air space among the bread cubes—not too much, though, so the stuffing will remain fairly light and fluffy. Drizzle with olive oil. Bake until top is golden brown, about 20 minutes.

GREEK GEMISTA

A lot of cultures, including virtually all the ones I like best, have a tendency to stuff things like bell peppers. But no culture can out-stuff the Greeks, who even call their popular summertime vegetable dish gemista, meaning essentially "stuff that is stuffed." Of course, I like it just fine when the stuffing incorporates ground beef or lamb, but if you don't use meat, you definitely won't miss it here.

Ingredients — Serves 6

6 large tomatoes
6 large green bell peppers
1 cup uncooked short grain rice
8 zucchini
1 onion
7 garlic cloves
2 pounds potatoes
1 tablespoon oregano

2 tablespoons dry mint
4 tablespoons fresh parsley
1 tablespoon tomato paste
¼ teaspoon ground cloves
¼ teaspoon ground allspice
1 ½ cups olive oil
Lemon juice
Salt and pepper

Preheat oven at 400° F. Wash the tomatoes and peppers. For the peppers, cut around the stem and empty the inside of the pepper. For the tomatoes cut around the base and empty the tomato with a spoon into a separate bowl. Make tiny slits on the inside bottom of the peppers and tomatoes. Place the empty tomatoes and peppers along with their caps in a large pan about 3 inches deep. Peel and grate the zucchini; put the grated zucchini in another bowl. In a food processor, add an onion, 4-5 garlic cloves, about 1 teaspoon of olive oil and some salt. Pulse briefly until the mix is crumbly but not mushy. Add the onion mixture to the zucchini.

Dice a small green bell pepper and add to the zucchini mixture. Take a small potato and grate it, adding to the zucchini mixture. Now squeeze the juice from the tomatoes with your hands too and save in a separate bowl. At this point, you should have 3 bowls: one with tomato, one with zucchini-potato-onion mixture and one with tomato juice.

Cut the tomato in small pieces and mix it with the zucchini mixture. Add 1 tablespoon salt, dry mint, parsley and tomato paste. Add to the mixture 10 to 12 tablespoons short grain rice and 1 teaspoon lemon juice. Add ¾ cup olive oil. Let the mixture sit. Take the potatoes, peel them and cut them into quarters, place in a bowl. Take 3-4 zucchini, peel and slice and add to potatoes. Add ¾ cup olive oil, 1 tablespoon oregano, salt and 2 cloves garlic cut in small pieces. Mix well with your hands, then add the tomato juice.

Start filling the tomatoes and peppers with rice all the way to the top and close with their caps. Add the potatoes to the pan, making sure to place around the tomatoes and peppers so they don't slide in the tray. If there is any rice mixture left mix it with the quartered potatoes and add to the pan. Add cloves to the potatoes and sprinkle with allspice. Add about a cup of water to the pan. Bake in the oven for 15-20 minutes, then reduce to 320° F and bake for another 1½ hours. If you notice it getting dry, add a bit more water. By the end of cooking, the rice should be soft and mushy and the vegetables should be lightly speckled with char. Serve a mix of different gemista with potatoes and, if desired, extra cooked rice.

DEER LAKE LODGE RAWSTA

I'm a devotee of neither veganism nor "raw foods," not least because I love to cook. But I tasted this salad named Rawsta (short for raw pasta, not without a clever nod to the vegan Rastafarians of my beloved Jamaica) recently at Deer Lake Lodge in Montgomery, and the flavors were amazing. For this, we can thank "raw chef" April Reeder, who goes by the nom de cuisine Sweet Mama Ree. Thus, the flavoring for these raw vegetables is known officially as Sweet Mama's Sunshine Love Goddess Dressing.

DRESSING
½ cup tahini
½ cup coconut oil
½ cup Bragg's apple cider vinegar
½ cup water
½ cup nutritional yeast
2 tablespoons lemon juice
1 tablespoon pure Grade B maple syrup
2 cloves garlic
1 teaspoon Himalayan sea salt
½ teaspoon turmeric, root or powder

4 zucchini
1 cucumber
1 red bell pepper, chopped
3 green onions, chopped

Ingredients

Serves 4-6

Make the dressing by placing all ingredients in a food processor or blender, blending until smooth. Add a bit more water if dressing is thicker than you like it. One at a time, run the zucchini and cucumber through a turning slicer (sometimes called a "spiralizer," sold under different brand names. I bought mine online for $38). Take the long vegetable "spaghetti" and cut with scissors so it's easier to eat. Combine in a mixing bowl with the bell pepper and green onion. Toss with the dressing. Let sit for 10-15 minutes to let the flavors develop. Serve room temperature.

BACON MAC & FIVE CHEESES

I don't think the phrase "Everything Is Better With Bacon" was imprinted on any of the early Texas flags, for the Republic or for the state. But eating my way around both town and county, I think it might as well have been.

Ingredients

Serves
6-8

12 ounces pasta shells
3 tablespoons butter
4 green onions, thinly sliced
⅛ teaspoon garlic powder
¼ cup all-purpose flour
1 cup heavy cream
1 ½ cups milk
6 slices bacon, cooked, drained, crumbled
1 cup shredded mozzarella
1 cup Mexican four-cheese blend
Salt and pepper

TOPPING
1 cup soft bread crumbs
1 ½ to 2 tablespoons butter, melted

Cook pasta shells following package directions. Drain in a colander, rinse with hot water, and set aside. Heat oven to 350° F. Coat a 2 ½ quart baking dish with vegetable spray. In a saucepan, melt butter. Add the green onions and garlic powder. Cook, stirring, for about 1 minute. Add the flour and stir until well blended and smooth. Add the cream, milk and about ½ the bacon; cook, stirring, until thickened. Season to taste with salt and pepper.

Stir the mozzarella and about ½ the Mexican cheese blend into the sauce and continue cooking until cheese is melted. Combine the cheese sauce with the drained macaroni and spoon into the prepared baking dish. Sprinkle the remaining bacon evenly over the casserole and top with the remaining ½ cup of cheese. Toss bread crumbs with melted butter in a bowl and sprinkle over the casserole. Bake for 25 to 30 minutes, until lightly browned and bubbly. Top with green onions.

NEEDLESS COOKERY

It was the best of times, it was the worst of times…so it seemed when I, then food editor of the *Houston Chronicle*, put aside all ideas of convenience and value and actually tried to cook something that nobody cooks at home anymore. Something like, oh, corn dogs and fortune cookies.

In this country, there's one common reason some foods pass out of the home repertoire. Somebody came up with a technique—or, more likely, a machine—that makes the product with sufficient quality and quantity for our efforts at home to seem silly. The results are not only some tasty foods but also a universe of "branded" items that dominate their categories. In most cases, these recipes are not only impractical to cook at home but also so protected from industrial espionage that buying the product off the shelf remains our only refuge. In conversation, we call such classics by their dominant brand name, even when we're munching on cheaper knockoffs. We want Oreos, in other words, not what I once saw genericized as "chocolate cream-filled wafer sandwiches."

Making corn dogs from scratch proved an inspiration—you know, the kind that fills you with false pride and convinced you you can do pretty much anything. Vendors at fairs, rodeos and carnivals have all kinds of special equipment, but it proved no great shakes to knock out a simple cornmeal batter and use it for dunking jumbo hot dogs threaded onto bamboo skewers. You then merely fry the things at that magical 375° F.

The only problem: Our skewers caught on the side of the frying pan and held much of each corndog above the bubbling immersion it wanted so desperately. The solution: We broke off the skewers, letting each cornmeal Titanic slip beneath the hot oil waves. Dipped in ketchup, sided in macaroni and cheese made from a blue box, the homemade corndog was a complete, perhaps historic success. Surely a fortune cookie would be easier, right? A local chef assured me it would be, when I quizzed him toward the end of a dinner far too fancy for such thoughts. No, the chef hadn't made any himself.

Have you ever tried writing a fortune? It's kind of like making a wish—and then having to tell everybody. There's nothing like public scrutiny to keep your wishes both G-rated and boring. No wonder fortunes in Chinese restaurant sound as innocuous as they do.

More than writing the fortunes, making the cookies was a total disaster. They turned out to be too big, too thick, too bland, too sticky. I couldn't even figure out how to fold them right—an embarrassment, since I'd bought a whole box of models at the grocery. Even single one of those seemed mixed and fortuned and cooked and folded and even wrapped, for about $1 per box. And they were Made in the USA, taking away my only potential excuse: that oppressed child labor on the other side of some ocean was to blame.

The bad news: We never got a single fortune cookie that looked like anything better than a taco stuffed with paper. The good news: By the time we ate all our mistakes, and even learned they were pretty good dunked in the uncooked batter, it wasn't quite the worst dessert I'd ever taste. Which might be worth a "fortune" all by itself.

GIANT BEANS

I like the way the Greeks refer to these beans on menus as simply "giants." Still, whatever size bean you decide to use in this recipe, I can guarantee it'll taste better than just about any you've ever tasted before. You'll probably want to double the recipe and enjoy leftovers, which always taste better anyway.

Ingredients

Serves 4-6

1 pound Greek gigantes (or large limas), soaked for 12 hours, drained

¼ cup extra-virgin olive oil

1 large Spanish onion, finely chopped

4 cloves garlic, minced

1 (15-ounce) can chopped plum tomatoes, with liquid

2 cups water

2 tablespoons honey

¼ teaspoon ground cloves

Salt and freshly ground black pepper

3 tablespoons chopped fresh parsley leaves

Add the beans to a pot with enough cold water to cover well. Bring to a boil, lower the heat, cover, and simmer until just soft throughout but not quite cooked, approximately 50 to 80 minutes, depending on the beans. Drain and set aside. Preheat the oven to 325° F. Heat olive oil over medium heat in a Dutch oven. Add onion and cook until soft. Add the garlic and cook for 30 seconds. Add tomatoes and their liquid, 2 cups water, honey, cloves, salt and pepper and boil gently for 20 to 30 minutes or until it begins to thicken. Stir in the parsley and remove from heat.

Place the beans in an oven-proof dish, pour tomato mixture on top, stir and spread mixture out evenly. Bake 1 ½ to 2 hours, or until beans are soft. Check the dish during cooking and add a small amount of boiling water if needed. The dish will look crispy on top. Remove from the oven and let sit for 10 minutes before serving. Serve hot or at room temperature.

CARAMELIZED BRUSSELS SPROUTS

I have to thank Texas chefs and bacon for teaching me to love Brussels sprouts. That's the way they invariably made these pint-sized cabbages, until one day I realized they tasted like nothing but bacon—and that I really, finally, loved the taste of Brussels sprouts. I haven't cooked them with bacon since.

1 pound Brussels sprouts

3 tablespoons olive oil

1 tablespoon butter

Creole seasoning

Ingredients

Serves 4

Slice the Brussels sprouts in half and partially cook in salted boiling water until crisp-tender, about 10 minutes. Drain. Heat the oil and butter together in a saucepan and add dry Brussels sprout halves, letting them brown on one side before turning with a spatula or tongs. Cook until golden flecked with brown. Season to taste with Creole seasoning.

ORANGE-THYME BABY CARROTS

I don't remember liking carrots when I was growing up. But once I saw what a few wisely chosen other ingredients could do to their already-sweet natural flavors, I became quite the carrot fan.

Ingredients

1 pound baby carrots
2 tablespoons butter
⅓ cup brown sugar

1 cup orange juice
½ teaspoon dried thyme
Salt and pepper

Serves 4-6

Partially boil the carrots in water until crisp-tender, about 10 minutes. Transfer the carrots into a saucepan with the butter over medium-high heat, stirring until lightly caramelized. Add the brown sugar and stir briefly, then pour in the orange juice. Add the thyme. Cook until sauce is thickened, 8-10 minutes. Season to taste with salt and pepper.

PATATAS BRAVAS

First there was the Fiesta Brava, one of many phrases people in Spain use to describe bullfights. Now there's Patatas Bravas, one of many phrases the folks south of Texas use to describe potatoes. And trust me, a couple forkfuls of these and you'll be fluent in any language you choose.

Ingredients

1 pound small new potatoes
  (about 1" diameter)
1 clove garlic, chopped
¼ teaspoon ground cumin
1 dried New Mexico chile, seeded
  and broken into pieces
½ teaspoon smoked hot Spanish paprika

1 teaspoon red or white wine vinegar
1 tablespoon olive oil
½ red or green bell pepper, seeded
  and sliced
2 tablespoon dark beer
Salt to taste

Serves 6

Boil potatoes until tender, about 10 minutes. Drain and quarter. Using a blender or small food processor grind together garlic, cumin, chilies and paprika. Add vinegar. Heat olive oil over medium high heat. Add potatoes and bell pepper, and brown potatoes. Add beer and cook until almost dry. Stir in vinegar/spice mixture, taking care to coat all potatoes. Add salt to taste and serve.

TWO HUNGRY TEXAS BOYS

The opening sequence rolls on televisions across America. Ah, it's *Cucina Amore*, that Italian cooking show, the one that made good-looking bearded Nick Stellino in his silky ascot a foodie celeb for three seasons. If memory doesn't quite serve, there are other none-too-subtle cues on the screen: Italian music, Italian food and two guys so obviously well-fed and boisterous that, even as mere images under theme music, they have to be Italian, too.

With their love-of-life meters set on overdrive, the two debuting hosts of *Cucina Amore* at last welcome their audience—speaking about Italian food through nothing less than the yellow "nose" of Texas. *Mama mia,* it's a *twang!*

"This Italian guy called me from Brooklyn once," Damian Mandola tells me a few nights after the TV premiere, over a dizzying spread of sausage and peppers, fried calamari and pizza margherita, all washed down with red wine at the original Carrabba's restaurant in Houston. "And he just couldn't believe it. He says to me, 'I've never heard Italian with a Texas accent before.' So I say right back, 'I've never heard Italian with a Brooklyn accent before.'"

That dinner with Damian and his cousin/partner in crime Johnny Carrabba proved to be life-changing for me in more ways than one. Well, okay, it was actually *dinners,* since we ate and drank ourselves silly at Carrabba's then walked around the corner to what was then their brand-new seafood place called Pesce, where we ate and drank ourselves silly all over again. It was also, though I'd been food editor of the *Houston Chronicle* only a few months, an audition. Before the night was over, I'd apparently passed, being invited by "the boys" to write the cookbooks that accompanied each season of their TV series. If I'd had my druthers, we'd still be doing TV and cranking out cookbooks, since Damian and Johnny became not only my friends but my heroes.

How could I know that, in short order, I would trade listening with glee to their Texas-sized repartee to writing the lines they would riff through, with no shortage of high-octane improv, on national television.

"Well, they were looking for a change," Johnny says of *Cucina Amore's* producers.

"Yeah," adds Damian, playing for me, his audience of one. "And I'm always the optimist. He's always the pessimist."

"At least," Johnny fires back, "at least I didn't go seven figures over budget on our new restaurant."

"So I wanted a little marble…"

"A little?"

And they were off, two of the larger-than-life characters who have enriched my live and expanded my waistline in almost equal proportions. They didn't really need cameras or booms or gaffers or best boys to do *Cucina*, whose first twenty-six episodes would air via PBS stations and slowly start replacing the show's original title with the Texas-friendly *Ciao, Y'all*. We featured the cuisine of Sicily the following season, which seemed logical considering it's the origin of most Gulf Coast Italians.

For the third season, when internal enthusiasm had started to lag, we focused on Tuscany, with me volunteering to spend a lot of my smallish fee from the production company to actually go to Tuscany and collect recipes. Up until then, my only travel for the show had been to my computer and back. I brought back more than a hundred Tuscan classics, some scribbled in pencil by taxi drivers, and then worked with Damian to cook each and every one. Before my eyes, he made each and every one *better.*

I'd never watched a flavor genius at work with such day-to-day, totally freeform intensity, and my own cooking changed forever as a result. Before long, I was cooking by all of Damian's rules, from "Always caramelize everything" to his mantra-to-end-all-mantras, "Never throw away flavor."

As that very first interview winds down over *vin santo* at Pesce, Damian ponders the success that has followed him since opening a small Italian restaurant in Huntsville with roommates at Sam Houston State. "After all this, people are saying I ought to slow down," he tells me. "And sometimes I think maybe they're right. But I still want to do my deli. I still want to do my casual place. I say: Let's do it. Let's do *it all*!"

Johnny nudges me with his elbow, gently, winking, "What are we gonna do with this guy, huh?"

SAN ANTONIO SQUASH CASSEROLE

The taste of Tex-Mex is so wonderful on so many meats and so many seafoods that we sometimes forget to apply the same ideas to our vegetables. After trying this casserole, that's not likely to be a mistake you make again.

Ingredients

Serves 10-12

2 ounces butter, divided, plus more for pan
2 cups diced yellow onion
2 pounds sliced yellow squash
½ pound cubed cheddar cheese

½ pound Monterey or pepper jack cheese
8 ounces canned diced green chiles
10 ounces cream of celery soup
¾ cup bread crumbs

Preheat oven to 350° F. Melt half of the butter in a large skillet over medium heat. Add onion and sauté until soft. In a separate skillet, sauté the squash in the remaining butter until soft. Alternatively, you can cook the squash in the microwave. Drain excess liquid from squash. Butter a casserole dish and then combine the onion, squash, cheese, green chiles and soup in the casserole dish. Bake until heated through and cheese is well melted. Remove from oven, stir, and sprinkle bread crumbs on top. Return to the oven and bake 5 more minutes, or until bread crumb mixture is golden.

CURRIED CAULIFLOWER & PEAS

Because I usually serve this vegetable dish alongside chicken curry (my version of Chicken Tikka Masala, the "national dish" of Great Britain), I want it to taste different from that. So out goes the tomato base; in comes an equally complex blend of Indian spices. Of course, you can serve this over basmati rice all by itself and not feel like you're missing out.

Ingredients

Serves 4-6

1-2 tablespoons extra-virgin olive oil
½ teaspoon crushed red pepper
1 onion, sliced in thin strips
2 cups cauliflower florets
1 teaspoon minced garlic
¼ cup chicken stock or water, as needed
¾ cup frozen green peas
1 tablespoon Patak's mild curry paste

1 teaspoon curry powder
½ teaspoon ground turmeric
½ teaspoon ground cumin
½ teaspoon onion powder
½ teaspoon garlic powder
Salt and freshly ground black pepper to taste
1-2 Roma tomatoes, chopped
¼ cup whole milk

Heat the oil with the crushed red pepper in a large skillet or wok. Add the onion and stir over medium-high heat until lightly caramelized, then add the cauliflower. As the florets start to turn golden around the edges, add the minced garlic and cook 1-2 minutes. Do not burn garlic. Add the chicken stock or water and cover for 2-3 minutes to cook cauliflower through. Stir in the green peas and cook 1 minute. Add the spices, starting with the curry paste, then curry powder, turmeric, cumin, onion and garlic powders, stirring to incorporate. Season to taste with salt and pepper. Add the chopped tomatoes and the milk, cooking just until tomatoes turn bright red and milk thickens into a light but creamy reddish-yellow sauce. Serve with basmati rice.

TOMATO RISOTTO

Throughout the quarter-century *Delicious Mischief* has sent me out into the world, I've discovered that one of the joys of living and especially of eating is risotto. I'm not sure too many Americans had ever heard of the stuff when the show went on the air, and now you see people everywhere ordering it in restaurants and even cooking it at home. Like most dishes, it isn't as complicated as it seems.

Ingredients

Serves 6-8

1 tablespoon extra-virgin olive oil
1 onion, finely chopped
Salt
Freshly ground white pepper
Freshly ground black pepper
6 cups water
2 teaspoons chopped garlic
2 cups Arborio rice

½ pound cherry tomatoes, cut in half
1 tablespoon butter
¼ cup heavy cream
½ cup freshly grated Parmesan cheese
2 tablespoons chopped green onions, green part only
2 tablespoons finely chopped fresh basil

Heat the oil in a large sauté pan. Add the onions. Season with salt and pepper, and cook, stirring. Sauté until the onions are slightly soft, about 3 minutes. Add the water and garlic. Bring the mixture to a boil, reduce the heat to medium, and simmer for about 6 minutes. Add the rice and simmer for 10 minutes, stirring constantly. Add the tomatoes and continue to simmer, stirring constantly, until the mixture is creamy and bubbly, about 8 minutes. Stir in the butter, cream, cheese, green onions and basil. Simmer for 2 minutes, stirring constantly. Remove from the heat. Spoon the risotto into serving bowls and garnish with slices of Parmesan.

BACON-JALAPEÑO CORN MAQUE CHOUX

Tasting the corn dish Del Frisco's Double Eagle Steak House served at the 2014's Best Bites competition in Houston inspired us so much that we reached into our own South Louisiana bag o' tricks and came up with our version.

½ pound bacon, chopped
6 ears young sweet corn
2 tablespoons vegetable oil
1 ½ cups chopped onions
1 cup chopped green bell peppers
1 tablespoon chopped jalapeños, or to taste

Salt
Ground red pepper
2 cups chopped, peeled and seeded tomatoes, or 1 cup chopped canned tomatoes
1 cup milk
¼ cup chopped green onions

In a large skillet, over medium heat, render the bacon until crispy. Drain the bacon on paper towels and set aside. Pour off all of the bacon fat except for 2 tablespoons. Cut the corn off the cob by thinly slicing across the tops of the kernels and then cutting across a second time to release the milk from the corn. Scrape the cob once or twice to extract the milk. You should have about 4 cups of corn with the milk. Add the oil, onions, bell peppers and jalapeños to the pan over medium heat. Sauté for 2 minutes. Add the corn. Season with salt and ground red pepper. Continue to sauté for 10 minutes. Add the tomatoes and cook, stirring occasionally, for 15 minutes, or until the corn is tender. Stir in the milk and remove from heat. Stir in the crispy bacon and green onions.

DESSeRTS

MARGARITA CAKE

Here in Texas, it's common to enjoy a margarita at the start of dinner. This sheet cake allows us to enjoy a margarita at the end of dinner as well.

Ingredients

Serves 18

CAKE
Cooking spray
2 tablespoons all-purpose flour
4 cups all-purpose flour
1 teaspoon baking powder
1 teaspoon baking soda
1 teaspoon salt
3 cups granulated sugar
1 cup unsalted butter, softened
6 large eggs
2 cups buttermilk
2 tablespoons finely grated lime rind
2 tablespoons fresh lime juice
2 teaspoons añejo tequila

ICING
6 cups powdered sugar
½ cup unsalted butter, softened
2 tablespoons lime zest
½ cup fresh lime juice
2 teaspoons añejo tequila
Additional lime zest for garnish

Preheat oven to 350° F. To prepare cake, coat a 12x16-inch sheet cake pan with cooking spray; line the bottom with wax paper. Coat wax paper with cooking spray. Dust pan with 2 tablespoons flour. Spoon 2 cups flour into dry measuring cups, and level with a knife. Combine 2 cups flour, baking powder, baking soda, and salt, stirring with a whisk. Place granulated sugar and ½ cup butter in a large bowl; beat with a mixer at medium speed until well blended, about 5 minutes.

Add eggs, one at a time, beating well after each addition. Add flour mixture and buttermilk alternately to sugar mixture, beginning and ending with the flour mixture. Beat in 2 tablespoons lime rind, lime juice and tequila. Pour batter into prepared pan; sharply tap pan once on counter to remove air bubbles. Bake for 35-40 minutes, or until a wooden pick inserted in center comes out clean. Cool in pan 10 minutes; remove from pan. Cool completely on wire rack; remove wax paper from cake.

To prepare icing, combine powdered sugar and the remaining ingredients in a large bowl; stir with a whisk until smooth. Carefully turn so cake is crust-side down onto a serving platter; spread icing on top of cake. Garnish with lime zest, if desired.

ROYER'S JUNKBERRY PIE

Around the Royer family's café in Round Top, many employees follow Bud the Pie Man's lead by unofficially calling this one not Junkberry but Crackberry. The filling recipe is enough for two pies. "Trust me," says Bud Royer, "you would regret not having two pies because this is like a drug."

CRUST
¼ teaspoon salt
1 cup milk
2 cups minus 3 tablespoons
   Crisco Shortening (blue label)
5 cups flour

FILLING
1 ½ cups sugar
¾ cup flour
2 Granny Smith apples, peeled,
   cored and sliced
2 cups frozen blueberries
1 cup frozen raspberries
2 cups frozen strawberries

3 cups frozen peaches
2 cups frozen blackberries

TOPPING
1 cup sour cream
¼ teaspoon salt
1 cup flour
1 ¼ cups sugar

Start making the crust by dissolving the salt in the milk, then cutting the shortening into the flour. Work the flour mixture together with the milk mixture until liquid is absorbed. If needed, add several tablespoons of flour and continue working the dough until it pulls away from your hands. Divide dough into 3 equal balls. Roll out dough to form thin circles.

When ready to make some pie, preheat oven to 350° F. Combine the sugar, flour, apples, blueberries, raspberries, strawberries, peaches and blackberries in a large saucepan. Bring to a boil, then pour this filling into one of the unbaked pie shells you've made from a ball of dough. Make the topping by mixing the sour cream with the salt, flour and sugar. Spread the topping over the fruit filling and sprinkle with additional sugar. Bake for 50 minutes. Topping should be firm and golden brown around the edges. Serve pie wedges warm with vanilla ice cream.

TRES LECHES

Legend has it that the original recipe for "three milks" was created as a way to "help" home cooks across Central America use more sweetened condensed milk; it was even printed on the label of the can. These days, tres leches is as likely to come from the pastry chef of a fancy restaurant as from Mama in her kitchen. Either way, count us in!

1 ½ cups all-purpose flour
1 teaspoon baking powder
½ cup unsalted butter
1 cup sugar
5 eggs
½ teaspoon vanilla extract
1 cup whole milk
7 ounces sweetened condensed milk
6 ounces evaporated milk

TOPPING
¾ cup evaporated milk
1 teaspoon vanilla extract
1 cup sugar

Ingredients

Serves 6-8

Preheat the oven to 350° F. Grease and flour a 9x13-inch baking pan. Sift together the flour and baking powder. Cream together the butter and sugar until fluffy. Add the eggs and vanilla, beating well. Add the flour mixture to the butter mixture a little at a time, mixing until incorporated. Pour into the prepared pan and bake for 30 minutes. Let cool. Pierce the cake with a fork in about 10 places. In a bowl, combine the milk, condensed milk and evaporated milk and pour over the cake. Refrigerate for 2 hours before serving. To make the topping, whip together all ingredients until thick and spread over the top of the chilled cake.

VENICE FOR VALENTINE'S

If you conspire with Fate, as Omar Khayyam used to put it, to have one more grand romance in your life, then it had better involve some*one.* But, equally it seems, it had better involve some*place.* For on that first Valentine's Day together, you'll want to be in the most romantic city on earth. It's a place whose natural and manmade beauties, whose bittersweet poetry of aging mixed with timelessness, and whose extraordinary gifts of history, art, literature, music, food and wine make it somewhere that more than a few poets have wished they could die happy.

Yes, for me, that would have to be Venice.

You have traveled to Venice the way Hemingway once wrote that he traveled to Paris, at every season of the year, by every conceivable mode of conveyance, single and married and single again, in a group and absolutely alone. You have been happy and sad in Venice, though always pleased to be there, and you've been treated to some of the most luxurious hotels and restaurants in this strangely "Oriental" city without ever forgetting the $5-a-day Locanda Rossi in 1974, your very first visit in the icy grip of winter, and therefore by definition the one you can never hope to equal.

Today, if you fly into Venice's Marco Polo International Airport, if you ride a train across the trestle that reaches out from the Italian mainland, or if (perhaps most appropriately) you watch Venice rise from the Adriatic like your favorite Botticelli painting, you think one thing first, last and always: The place doesn't *look* like Europe. And there's a good reason for that. In the 13th century, when the Serene Republic, to be called *Venezia,* started forming from tribes and villages spread across 117 tiny islands, the future lay not in the struggling medieval West but in the exotic East. Marco Polo was drinking the local water, after all.

For at least a day or two, you'll want to remain close to Piazza San Marco. This is the heartbeat. In the summer a quagmire of endless lines to enter the Basilica, the Piazza in winter is more sedate, more beloved. On icy days, you love the way the cobblestones get wet and glaze over, adding to the city's eternal shimmer and making for pigeons that walk like they're drunk.

In terms of Venetian history, St. Mark's Basilica has it all, starting in 828 AD when a gang of merchants claimed to have smuggled the namesake evangelist's bones out of Egypt. Though the Church fathers (yes, far away in Rome) took a dim view, Venice continued to pat itself on the back every time it praised God, pulling together pieces for an East-Meets-West palace of worship unlike anything else in Christendom.

As the hours and days in Venice flow by, you venture forth from the Piazza— sometimes no farther than the Doge's Palace with its iconic arcades and the Bridge of Sighs, so named by Lord Byron in one of his more fanciful moments. According to local legend, everlasting love awaits couples who kiss in a gondola beneath the Bridge of Sighs at sunset. At least the gondoliers union would say so. Farther away, there's the Accademia for great paintings you sort-of recognize from art history in college, Teatro La Fenice for operas and chamber music (Venice loves chamber music, going back to the days Vivaldi slept here), the district around the Rialto Bridge for seafood, fresh fruits and vegetables and even mops and buckets in the morning, and the fascinating Jewish Ghetto.

Venice is a world of shadowy no-name churches with great paintings, of tiny squares you never heard of that break your heart with beauty, of restaurants, trattorias, pizzerias and cafes that welcome you (especially removed from tourist season), and of the thousand routes you might decide to walk from one place to the next and on from there. You may or may not have something resembling a GPS; but this Venice of past grandeur, present intrigue and future promise would surely baffle any device anyway. On *this* visit to la Serenissima, on *this* special Valentine's Day, you'd be safer following your heart.

KEY LIME CRÈME BRULEE

For years I suggested to pastry chefs I knew, without any hope of personal fame or fortune, that they make this dessert. Oddly enough, I'm not sure that any of them ever did. I am sure that I started making it myself and therefore don't need them quite so much anymore.

Ingredients

Serves 8

8 egg yolks
½ cup sugar
2 ½ cups heavy cream
¼ cup key lime juice

1 tablespoon vanilla extract
1 teaspoon lime zest
3 tablespoons dark brown sugar

Preheat oven to 250° F. In a bowl, mix the egg yolks and sugar until just combined. In a saucepan, heat the cream to just below a simmer; add to yolk mixture gradually, beating constantly. Stir in the lime juice. Continue to beat until mixture is smooth. Pass through a fine strainer into a bowl or measuring cup with a pouring lip. Stir in vanilla and zest. Pour into 8 ramekins. Place the ramekins in a large baking pan. Add water to the pan until it reaches halfway up the side of the ramekins. Bake until set but still jiggly, about 45 minutes. Do not overbake. Remove ramekins from pan. Cool to room temperature and then refrigerate 8 hours or up to 2 days. Before serving, top each custard with brown sugar. Using a small torch, crisp and caramelize the brown sugar.

FLOURLESS CHOCOLATE-PECAN CAKE

I'd always enjoyed flourless chocolate cakes in restaurants, but I'd never quite gotten around to making one—until now. The request came in for a party I was cooking for, and while I don't consider myself a baker, I definitely was excited about the challenge. Turns out, as any chocoholic will tell you, you don't have to do that much to chocolate to make people love it.

1 cup (2 sticks) unsalted butter, cut into pieces, plus additional
⅓ cup unsweetened cocoa powder, plus additional
1 ½ cups heavy cream
8 ounces bittersweet chocolate, chopped
6 large eggs

1 cup granulated sugar
1 cup crushed Texas pecans
2 tablespoons Cognac or other brandy
1 teaspoon vanilla extract
½ teaspoon almond extract
¼ cup confectioners sugar

SAUCE
1 cup raspberries
¼ cup granulated sugar
½ cup water
½ cup Cognac or other brandy

Serves 10-12

Preheat oven to 350° F. Butter a 9-inch Springform pan and dust with cocoa powder. In a medium saucepan, melt the butter with 1 cup heavy cream. Add the chocolate pieces and stir until thoroughly melted. Remove from heat. In a medium bowl, whisk together the eggs, granulated sugar and cocoa powder. Whisk in the melted chocolate mixture, followed by the pecans, 1 tablespoon Cognac, vanilla and almond. Pour the batter into the prepared pan and bake until set, 40-45 minutes. Let cool in pan for 1 hour, then run knife around the edges and invert onto a serving dish.

To make whipped cream, pour the remaining heavy cream and confectioners sugar into a chilled metal bowl and beat with a chilled metal whisk, until thickened with soft peaks forming. Whisk in remaining cognac.

To make the sauce, stir the raspberries with the sugar and water over medium-high until bubbly, then carefully pour in the Cognac and flambé until the flame burns out. Spoon raspberries and sauce over wedges of cake. Top with whipped cream.

BANANAS FOSTER BREAD PUDDING

Have you ever been there in New Orleans facing life's ultimate quandary: whether to order bread pudding or bananas Foster for dessert? Well, I have. And I set out to make that a quandary no more.

Ingredients

Serves 16-18

1 ½ sticks unsalted butter
1 ½ cups brown sugar
1 teaspoon ground cinnamon
7 ripe bananas, sliced into coins
½ cup banana liqueur
½ cup dark rum
5 eggs, beaten
3 cups heavy cream
1 cup whole milk
1 teaspoon vanilla extract

1 teaspoon almond extract
⅛ teaspoon salt
7 cups cubed day-old French bread

SAUCE
¾ cup sugar
1 tablespoon water
½ teaspoon lemon juice
½ cup heavy cream

Preheat the oven to 350° F. Butter a large 10x14-inch baking dish. Then, make traditional Bananas Foster: Melt the butter in a large saucepan. Stir in 1 cup of the brown sugar and the cinnamon, stirring until smoothly incorporated. Add the bananas and cook just until soft, depending on their degree of ripeness. Stir in the banana liqueur, then carefully add the rum and flame until the fire burns out. Let mixture cool.

In a large bowl, mix together the eggs, the remaining ½ cup brown sugar, cream, milk and vanilla and almond extracts. Add the cooled banana mixture and incorporate. Add the cubed French bread and press into the liquid until all cubes are soaked. Transfer to the buttered baking dish. Bake until firm and golden brown on top, about 1 hour. Cool for about 20 minutes before serving.

Meanwhile, prepare the sauce. Combine the sugar with the water and lemon juice in a heavy saucepan. Stir over medium-high heat until all sugar is dissolved, then allow to bubble without stirring until the mixture turns golden. Don't let it burn. Stir in the cream, being careful not to splatter, until the sauce is smooth. Drizzle over the slightly cooled bread pudding and serve in squares.

HILL COUNTRY PEACH BISCOTTI CRUMBLE

Here's a fun dessert I've been making for a few years—very much Tuscany by way of Texas. You can, of course, form the things in individual molds and make them look all fancy, which I've done. But I kind of prefer the crumble approach. This is a great way to welcome each peach season around Fredericksburg and Stonewall in the Hill Country.

Ingredients

Serves 6-8

4-5 five fresh Texas peaches, peeled, pitted and sliced (or frozen peach slices)
2 tablespoons plus 1 tablespoon unsalted butter
2 tablespoons brown sugar
½ teaspoon ground cinnamon
¼ cup rum

8 biscotti, broken into chunks
1 cup whipping cream
2 tablespoons powdered sugar
2 tablespoon Texas Muscat Canelli dessert wine

Combine the sliced peaches with 2 tablespoons butter, brown sugar and cinnamon in a sauté pan and stir over medium heat until the peaches start to soften, 4-5 minutes. Flame the peaches with the rum. When the alcohol has burned off, pour the peaches into a casserole dish with the broken-up biscotti and combine, letting the biscotti soak up the peach liquid. Press down lightly in the casserole and dot with pieces of the remaining butter.

Set in a preheated 350° F oven and bake until golden on top, about 15 minutes. Meanwhile, using a chilled whisk in a chilled stainless steel mixing bowl, beat the cream with the sugar and wine until peaks form. To serve, spoon warm peach crumble onto dessert plates and top with chilled whipped cream.

GERMAN'S CHOCOLATE CAKE

Everybody has a favorite cake, right—the kind they wish they'd have for every birthday? Well, mine has always been German chocolate. And I've always wondered, every time I enjoy a slice, what's so "German" about sweetened flaked coconut and chopped pecans. It turns out that German chocolate cake isn't from Germany at all. It got its name from a mid-19th-century brand of American sweet chocolate developed by a fellow named Sam German and called for in a cake recipe published in a Dallas newspaper in 1957. The possessive simply got lost over the decades since then. Consoled by that knowledge, I can finally eat my favorite cake in peace.

Ingredients

Serves 12

CAKE

Vegetable shortening or spray
All-purpose flour
2 ½ cups cake flour
1 teaspoon baking powder
½ teaspoon salt
½ cup water
4 (1-ounce) squares German's sweet chocolate
1 cup butter, softened
2 cups sugar
4 eggs, separated
1 teaspoon vanilla extract
½ teaspoon almond extract
1 cup buttermilk

FILLING

1 cup sugar
1 cup evaporated milk
½ cup butter
3 egg yolks
1 ⅓ cups flaked coconut
1 cup chopped pecans
1 teaspoon coconut extract
1 teaspoon vanilla extract

Preheat the oven to 350° F. Generously coat 3 9-inch round cake pans with shortening or spray and then all-purpose flour. In a bowl, sift together the cake flour, baking powder and salt. Heat the water and chocolate in a small saucepan, stirring until melted and combined. Allow to cool. In a large bowl, cream the butter with the sugar until fluffy. Beat in the egg yolks one at a time. Blend in the melted chocolate along with the vanilla and almond extracts. Alternating, beat in the flour mixture and the buttermilk, mixing each time just until incorporated.

Beat the egg whites in a large glass or metal mixing bowl until stiff peaks form. Fold about one-third of the whites into the batter followed by the rest, folding until no white streaks remain. Pour the batter in the pan and bake until a toothpick inserted in the center comes out clean, about 30 minutes. Cool in the pan for 10 minutes then invert onto wire racks. While cakes are cooling completely, make the filling by combining the sugar, evaporated milk, butter and egg yolks in a saucepan. Stirring constantly, cook over low heat until thickened. Stir in the coconut, pecans, vanilla and coconut extracts. Cool until thickened more. Assemble the three layers with filling between each and on top.

CHEESECAKE *on a* STICK

What is it about Texans that we love any food we can possibly put on a stick? You'd think we'd be wary of this arguably foreign practice, evoking as it does the skewered meats of Persia and the Middle East that get grouped under the name shish kebab. But no, we love everything on a stick, especially with some fair, festival or rodeo as the world's most natural side dish. There's an unlimited collection of possible coatings—which means that in Texas most cheesecakes on a stick come out chocolate, pretty much like these.

Ingredients

Makes 12

CRUST
1 cup Graham cracker crumbs
½ cup chopped pecans
½ cup melted butter

FILLING
2 (8-ounce) packages cream cheese, softened
½ cup sugar
¼ cup sour cream
½ teaspoon vanilla extract
½ teaspoon almond extract
2 eggs

COATING
24 ounces semi-sweet chocolate, chopped
3 tablespoons shortening

Preheat the oven to 300° F. Line an 8-inch square baking pan with aluminum foil to extend over the sides of the pan. Spray foil with cooking spray. Mix the crust ingredients in a small bowl and press into the bottom of the lined pan. Set in oven for about 8 minutes. Let cool.

Meanwhile, beat the cream cheese in a large bowl, then add the remaining Filling ingredients and beat until smooth. Pour Filling over cooled crust and bake until edges are set, about 45 minutes. Soft center will set as the cake cools. Refrigerate 1 ½ hours then freeze until firm, about 2 hours. Remove cheesecake from the pan by lifting and removing the foil. Cut into 3 equal strips. Then, by shifting the knife angle back and forth, cut the strips into triangles resembling Christmas trees. Insert wooden "popsicle" sticks into bottom of each tree.

Working quickly, while cheesecake is still mostly frozen, melt the chocolate and shortening together in a saucepan, stirring frequently. Cool slightly, 2-3 minutes, then pour into a glass 2-cup measuring cup. Holding by the stick, dip each triangle into the melted chocolate to cover the bottom and sides. Let any excess chocolate drip off. Return to waxed paper and set in the freezer for at least 30 minutes.

PIÑA COLADA CHEESECAKE

All my adult life, it seems, I'd fantasized about a cheesecake that mimicked the better aspects of a piña colada. Eventually, I made my fantasy a reality, as one is allowed to do every so often.

Ingredients

Serves 8

CRUST
1 cup graham cracker crumbs
4 tablespoons sweetened flaked coconut
2 tablespoons granulated sugar
4 tablespoons melted butter

FILLING
3 (8-ounce) packages cream cheese, softened
1 cup granulated sugar
1 tablespoon cornstarch
4 eggs
⅓ cup canned Coco Lopez or coconut milk, stirred
2 tablespoons pineapple juice
1 tablespoon coconut extract
1 teaspoon vanilla extract
1 teaspoon almond extract
Flaked coconut for garnish

SAUCE
¼ cup brown sugar
4 tablespoons unsalted butter
1 (8-ounce) can crushed pineapple
¼ cup pineapple juice
¼ cup golden rum

Preheat oven to 325° F. Set a large, shallow pan of water in the bottom of the oven. Prepare the crust by covering the bottom of a 9-inch springform pan with vegetable spray. In a mixing bowl, combine all crust ingredients, tossing until crumbs are moistened. Press into the bottom of the pan and bake 8 minutes. Cool completely.

Lower the oven temperature to 250° F. Beat the cream cheese, sugar and cornstarch with a mixer in a large bowl until light and fluffy. Beat in the eggs 1 at a time. Beat in the coconut milk, the juice and the extracts until smooth. Pour filling into crust. Bake until set but still jiggly, about 1 ¼ hours. Turn off oven but leave cheesecake with door closed for 1 hour more, then chill in the refrigerator at least 4 hours, preferably overnight.

Run a knife around the edge of the cake, then loosen the pan to release. Press coconut flakes along side of cake. Make the sauce by melting the butter with the brown sugar until smooth, then stir in crushed pineapple and juice. Cook for about 2 minutes. Flame with rum, letting fire burn out. Bubble until syrupy, about 2 minutes more. Cut the cheesecake and top with sauce and additional coconut.

TEXAS DEWBERRY COBBLER

For the briefest of times each summer, Texas is all about the dewberry. Sure, it's more or less like a blackberry, and certainly blackberries can be used happily in any dewberry recipe. But dewberries remain a vivid part of any Texan's birthright.

2 ¼ cups all-purpose flour
1 teaspoon salt
¾ cup shortening
2 eggs, beaten
¼ cup milk

5 cups fresh Texas dewberries or blackberries
2 cups sugar
2 tablespoons butter
Vanilla ice cream

Ingredients

Serves
8

Combine flour and salt in a large mixing bowl, stirring well; cut in shortening with a pastry blender until mixture resembles coarse meal. Add eggs and milk; stir with a fork just until dry ingredients are moistened. Turn out onto a heavily floured surface, and knead 2 or 3 times. Roll one-fourth of pastry on a floured surface into a 10x6-inch rectangle, and cut into 10x1-inch strips. Place strips on an ungreased baking sheet; bake at 450° F for 5 minutes. Let cool on baking sheet.

Divide remaining dough in half. Roll one half to ⅛-inch thickness on a lightly floured surface, and fit into a 10x6x2-inch baking dish. Set aside prepared dish and remaining portion of dough. Combine berries and sugar; toss lightly to coat well. Spoon half of berries evenly into prepared dish; carefully arrange baked pastry strips over top. Spoon remaining berries over strips; dot with butter.

Roll remaining dough to ¼-inch thickness on a floured surface. Carefully place over berries. Trim edges; seal and flute. Cut slits in top crust. Bake at 450° F for 20 minutes; reduce temperature to 350° F, and bake an additional 15 minutes or until golden brown. Serve warm, and top with ice cream.

PECAN PIE

I'm no slouch when it comes to sampling new, innovative and usually complicated desserts from some of the world's best pastry chefs. But if you ask what my favorite dessert of all time is, it always comes down to Texas pecan pie. For a dish with only seven ingredients, it's quite a life-changer.

Ingredients

Serves 8

1 cup corn syrup, such as Karo
3 eggs
1 cup sugar
2 tablespoons butter, melted

1 teaspoon pure vanilla extract
1 ½ cups (6 ounces) Texas pecans
1 (9-inch) unbaked or frozen deep-dish
  pie crust

Preheat oven to 350° F. Mix corn syrup, eggs, sugar, butter and vanilla using a spoon. Stir in pecans. Pour filling into pie crust. Bake on center rack of oven for 60 to 70 minutes. Cool for 2 hours on wire rack before serving.

NOTE: To use prepared frozen pie crust, place cookie sheet in oven and preheat oven as directed. Pour filling into frozen crust and bake on preheated cookie sheet.

WHITE CHOCOLATE-MACADAMIA HUMMUS

The first time my daughter asked me to think about making "dessert hummus," I thought she was nuts. I've made a lot of hummus in my life, from caramelized onion and tomato to black bean and corn to spicy roasted red pepper, but none of it tastes at all like dessert. Turns out, if you can set your preconceptions aside, there is something to this strange idea. This recipe makes a nice dessert with Graham crackers, or an even nicer breakfast.

Ingredients

1 cup chopped macadamia nuts
1 can chick peas (garbanzos), drained
4 tablespoons crunchy peanut butter
4 tablespoons honey
2 teaspoons vanilla extract

1 teaspoon almond extract
½ teaspoon salt
2 tablespoons whole milk
⅓ cup white chocolate chips
Graham crackers

Serves 6

Pour about half the macadamias into a food processor or blender, then pulse until the nuts are almost powdery. Add the drained chick peas, peanut butter and honey, processing until a smooth, thick mixture forms. Add more honey to taste, along with the vanilla, almond, salt and milk. Blend until incorporated. Adjust milk to your preferred consistency. Transfer to a serving bowl and fold in the remaining macadamia pieces and white chocolate chips. Serve with Graham crackers for dipping, or spread on the crackers.

GRANBURY FRENCH TOAST

I tasted this amazing dessert, breakfast or brunch dish at the Inn on Lake Granbury, a pampering small property within an easy stroll of Granbury's historic courthouse, central square and all the restaurants, coffee shops and boutiques spread around it. I can't think of a more festive way to start your morning.

Ingredients

8 pre-baked mini croissants
1 cup cream cheese, softened
1 cup crushed pineapple, drained with juice reserved, pineapple separated in half
4 eggs
1 ½ cups whole milk or half and half
⅓ cup plus ¼ cup sugar

½ teaspoon vanilla
¼ cup rum
½ cup unsalted butter
½ cup heavy cream
Sweetened shredded coconut

Serves 8

Preheat oven to 350º F. Spray bottom and sides of a baking dish. In a small bowl, mix cream cheese and half the crushed pineapple. Slice the croissants and spread inside with the cream cheese-pineapple mixture. Arrange the croissants on the baking dish so they overlap slightly. To prepare the custard, beat the eggs in a mixing bowl, then add the reserved pineapple liquid, milk, ⅓ cup sugar and vanilla. Pour over the croissants and let sit 15 minutes to soak.

Scatter the sweetened coconut over the top and take until custard is set, about 30 minutes. To make the sauce, combine the butter, rum, remaining sugar, heavy cream and remaining crushed pineapple in a saucepan and cook over medium-low heat until the sauce bubbles and thickens. Stir occasionally. (This can also be done in the microwave.) Serve with the French toast.

RAW CACAO BROWNIE BITES

As part of researching a radio show on juice fasts and "detox weekends," I certainly wasn't expecting one of my life's most intriguing encounters with chocolate. So it went with "raw chef" April Reeder at Deer Lake Lodge, who made us these rolled-up (and raw!) bites of cacao, peppermint and hemp.

Ingredients

Serves 24

1 ½ cups organic pitted dates (add to food processor until becomes a ball)
Put dates in metal bowl and everything mix
1 ½ chopped cups pecans
7 tablespoons raw cacao (cocoa) powder
5 tablespoons of raw hemp protein
2 tablespoons of flax or chia seeds

¼ teaspoon Real Salt
Inside resin of ½ of organic vanilla bean
4 tablespoons maple syrup
7-13 drops of pure organic food grade peppermint oil
6 tablespoons shredded unsweetened coconut

Run the dates through a food processor until they form a ball. Mix the dates with all remaining ingredients except coconut in a large bowl until it binds. Roll into individual bites the size of gold balls and roll in coconut flakes. Allow to the set on a cookie sheet in the refrigerator for about 30 minutes.

WINDOWS ON THE WORLD

As food editor of the *Houston Chronicle*, I couldn't help thinking about dinner. And it hurt to think about *this* dinner, even feeling my memory dragged back more than 20 years to my first and only meal at Windows on the World, the legendary restaurant on the 107th floor of the World Trade Center in New York.

Watching what I knew to be Windows crumbling into an avalanche of smoke and plummeting toward what would soon be known as Ground Zero, my first thought was of the employees. I thought of the employees because I couldn't *not* think of them, and slowly, a ray of hope sliced in. What if, I wondered, no workers were on duty yet? What if Windows opened only for dinner? If so, then only a tiny portion of a crew would have been there.

"No, John," a quiet voice on the phone stopped my wishful thinking. I had called a friend who had helped with the renovation of Windows in the mid-1990s. "They don't just serve dinner. And they don't just serve lunch and dinner. John, I'm sure they were busy with breakfast!" Of course. It was *New York*—home of the power breakfast. The only place on earth where business lunches and business dinners are not enough. Remembering Windows, its elegant dining rooms, its expensive dishes prepared by expensive chefs, its endless wine list...remembering Windows was too painful. But I kept remembering anyway.

I'd arrived in the afternoon, a young man with a job at the *Daily News* in Jackson, Mississippi, a young wife and, at that time, no children, probably attracted by some special deal. It was still daylight when I let the express elevator carry me higher than I've felt on most airplanes. It's the kind of height you feel more than see, especially as the changes in pressure beat drums inside your ears. I don't remember anything I ate, since I wasn't yet a "food guy." But I do remember the feeling. The sense of being surrounded by commerce, by lots of money. And I also remember feeling too high up, as though without thinking I'd climbed a mountain past some invisible point where anybody could ever reach up to save me.

At the time, I brushed that feeling aside, as I would later aboard ocean liners crossing the North Atlantic in storms, in cable cars stalled high above valleys on islands in the Indian Ocean, and far more often in planes at 38,000 feet. They *can* save you, I forced a voice inside me to intone. They can *always* save you. That day, my only real disappointment was the total absence of a view. It was a rainy day, and Windows on the World was perched within a thick carpet of clouds, which edged from gray toward black as late afternoon faded into evening.

All that dreary late afternoon, I scanned all the windows visible from my table, looking for some sign the weather was breaking. At one point I registered a distant blinking light or two, probably the top of the Empire State Building, or maybe the swirling Art Deco peak of the Chrysler Building. Or maybe something else altogether. The weather never broke, so it was impossible to know.

Making one final attempt before departing, I took a stroll the whole way around, searching for any view, any *thing* that might make me feel better. There was, at that moment, in the full 360 degrees, only one such break. And it peered down and down and down to what seemed to be a universe of black water. There was a form, now tiny, dark against dark, and a strange pinpoint of light somewhere above the form. It was my only view that day—the only view I'd ever have, as history dictated—from atop the World Trade Center.

Straining my eyes, I finally recognized the dark form so tiny against the expanse of dark water, with only that single pinpoint of light. It was, of course, the Statue of Liberty.

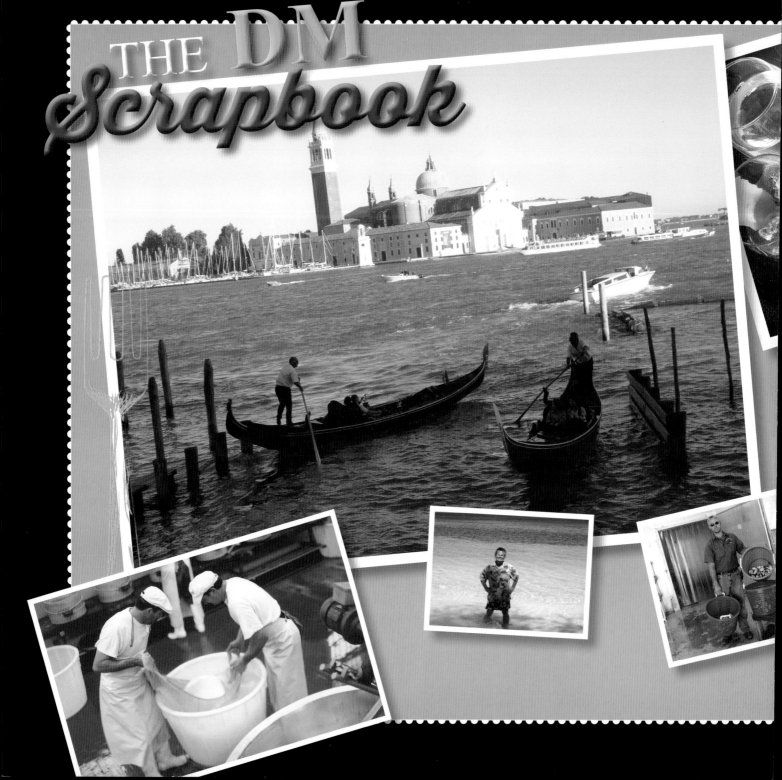

THE DM Scrapbook